Easy Diabetic Meal Prep 2019-2020

Simple and Healthy Recipes — 3 Weeks Meal Plan — Lower Blood Sugar and Reverse Diabetes

By Betty Moore

Copyrights©2019 By Betty Moore
All Rights Reserved

This document is geared towards providing exact and reliable information in regards to the topic and issue covered. The publication is sold with the idea that the publisher is not required to render accounting, officially permitted, or otherwise, qualified services. If advice is necessary, legal or professional, a practiced individual in the profession should be ordered.

Legal Notice:

The book is copyright protected. This is only for personal use. You cannot amend, distribute, sell, use, quote or paraphrase any part or the content within this book without the consent of the author.
Under no circumstance will any legal responsibility or blame be held against the publisher for any reparation, damages, or monetary loss due to the information herein, either directly or indirectly.

Disclaimer Notice:

Please note the information contained within this document is for educational and entertainment purpose only. Every attempt has been made to provide accurate, up to date and reliable complete information. No warranties of any kind are expressed or implied. Reader acknowledge that the author is not engaging in the rendering of legal, financial, medical or professional advice. The content of this book has been derived from various sources. Please consult a licensed professional before attempting any techniques outlined in this book.

table of Content

Introduction 1
Compartmentalizing Your Plate 3
Calories and Carbohydrates 3
Preparing Diabetic Meals 5
Smart Usage Of The Ingredients 5
Cook Now and Rest Later... 7
Finding your Rhythm 8
Storage Principles 8
What Can You Expect From This Book? 9

Breakfast Recipes 11
Herb & Vegetable Egg White Omelet 12
Lemon Chia Parfait with Berries 13
Whole Wheat Banana Cinnamon Pancakes 14
Denver Omelet Breakfast Salad 15
Fruit and Nut Granola 16
Easy Egg Scramble 17
Spiced Overnight Oats 18
Eggs Baked in Peppers 19
Spinach and Ham Egg Muffins 20
Banana Matcha Breakfast Smoothie 21
Cinnamon Oat Pancakes 22
Easy Vegetable Frittata 23
Vanilla Mixed Berry Smoothie 24

Lunch Recipes... 25
Asian Cold Noodle Salad... 26
Chicken Tortilla Soup 27
Turkey & Brown Rice Lettuce Cups 28
Shrimp and Black Bean Salad 29
Chicken, Spinach, and Pesto Soup 30
Creamy Broccoli Chickpea Salad 31
Chickpea, Tuna, and Kale Salad 32
Avocado Veggie Wrap 33
Grilled Avocado Hummus Paninis 34
Ceviche-Stuffed Avocado Halves.. 35
Carrot Ginger Soup 36
Avocado White Bean Sandwich 37
Turkey Cobb Salad 38

Dinner Recipes.. 39
Almond-Crusted Salmon 40
Chicken & Veggie Bowl with Brown Rice 41
Beef Fajitas 42

Sautéed Turkey Bowl 43
Chicken Mushroom Stroganoff 44
Grilled Tuna Kebabs 45
Cast-Iron Pork Loin 46
Crispy Baked Tofu 47
Tilapia with Coconut Rice 48
Spicy Turkey Tacos 49
Quick and Easy Shrimp Stir-Fry 50
Chicken Burrito Bowl with Quinoa 51
Baked Salmon Cakes 52

Snack & Dessert Recipes 53
Cinnamon Spiced Popcorn 54
Grilled Peaches 55
Peanut Butter Banana "Ice Cream" 56
Fruity Coconut Energy Balls 57
Mini Apple Oat Muffins 58
Dark Chocolate Almond Yogurt Cups 59
Chocolate Avocado Mousse 60
Pumpkin Spice Snack Balls 61
Strawberry Lime Pudding 62
Cinnamon Toasted Almonds 63
Grain-Free Berry Cobbler 64
Whole-Wheat Pumpkin Muffins 65

Side Dishes Recipe 66
Lemon Garlic Green Beans 67
Brown Rice & Lentil Salad 68
Mashed Butternut Squash 69
Cilantro Lime Quinoa 70
Oven-Roasted Veggies 71
Vegetable Rice Pilaf 72
Curry Roasted Cauliflower Florets 73
Mushroom Barley Risotto 74
Braised Summer Squash 75
Parsley Tabbouleh 76
Garlic Sautéed Spinach 77
French Lentils 78

21 Days Meal Plan 79

Introduction

How many times have you heard someone say that, whatever you feed this body, it is who you become? Well, if we follow this logic, then all the diabetic people must be some hyper-sweet people who are bereft of all the anger issues. But from what I have heard, they are not.

This means that being a diabetic is indeed a disease that has its own symptoms; it has its own identity and some specific side effects. So, to say that being a diabetic is nothing but a lifestyle or just a phase of life is not right. Instead, being a diabetic patient, and I would call them the patient is different because these are the people, who need a constant check on their health, their dietary itinerary, daily routine, and everything else.

I have been helping, supporting, and assisting people with diabetes for most of my life. And the only thing that I have learned in all these years is that diabetes can be treated, provided you have the right mix. This means there has to be a good synchronization between what you eat and when you eat it. And the reason why I am writing this book is to make sure that you get to know that combination.

This book is for all those people who want to adapt to a better lifestyle which is filled with physical fitness and mental stability. This relation of mental stability with diabetes is prominent because I have seen people hurting their psychological health due to the incidence of diabetes. They often relate everything with this condition and hence start living a life that feels like a burden and meaningless.

In medical languages, diabetes is not even called a disease or a condition; instead, it is called a disorder. And any that is disorderly can be brought on the right path provided you follow a set pattern of moves. In our case, this pattern will consist of the type of food you eat, when you eat it, and how you eat it. Also, what is the quantity, what has to be the quality and other such questions which need answering?

Diabetes can, indeed, be fatal. And that if it goes unchecked, the cumulative effect of this disorder would be like giving your health and life away to a small dysfunction inside your body. When we say that the body has a high amount of sugars, it means that the body of a person affected with diabetes cannot absorb the sugar that they ingest. We need to digest this sugar to make sure that the cells are getting the right amount of energy.

When you are suffering from this condition, your body does not produce insulin. The insulin is credited with the function of triggering a specific cohort of body cells to absorb the incoming sugars through the food we eat and drink. Now, if the insulin won't tell the beta cells to absorb the sugars, they won't do it. And failure to do so leads to an increase in the level of sugars in your blood.

If we go into the reasons for the development of diabetes in the first place, then various causes will come ashore. The most prominent of them is the food we eat. Earlier, the cases where children suffering from this condition was rare. But today, there are several children, especially in the developed nations who develop this disorder early on. The reason can be genetic, but at the back of this reason, too, there are parent's unhealthy eating habits. That is why the very first thing that we are going to talk about is how to divide your plate.

Compartmentalizing Your Plate

Considering that you eat on a round plate, you need to divide the circle into three parts. One segment will be for proteins, one will be for starch or grain-based food, and the last one will be for non-starchy vegetables.

There is a reason for this. Almost all types of food that we eat has some amount of sugar present in it. The amount may be negligible, but it is there. These are called the natural sugars which give the food its sweet taste. But there are other food items which are bereft of any kind of added or natural sugars. Take, for example, beef, lamb, chicken, pork, and a few other things.

If you are thinking of buying the canned versions of these foods, then don't. Because every canned food has some form of added sugars to it for preservation purposes, and if you stick to all the food items that have no natural or artificial sugar content, you will be giving birth to a lot many other issues.

That is the biggest irony that I have ever come across in my career. And this is why I think this book will suffice the needs of every person who wants to find the right mix of the food that they can eat without even checking their blood sugar levels every day.

And do you know why I chose this area of study? Well, for one, it is because I love food. Secondly, I wanted to help people make the right choice. And believe me when I say that people like me who really want to help people who are suffering are very rare to find. Through this book, I aim to assist and support every single patient with diabetes to get the best kind of help that they want. I want to make sure that you are getting to the top of your health even after suffering from such a condition that can just rile things up inside the body.

Calories and Carbohydrates

Let's talk about carbohydrates first. These are the nutrients that are also called simple sugars. Every single dietician will tell you to cut down on the carbs, especially complex carbohydrates, also called starch. When ingested, the intravenous system of the body will break them down into blood glucose. This glucose then increases the level of sugar in the blood, thus causing all the problems. And it is not that you can just stop eating all the carbs. That is never a good thing to do. Without them, you won't get any sort of energy. When it comes to having a balanced diet, every single nutrient is essential. You need to eat right and have the right quantity. That is why I always suggest my patients choose their carbs right.

In this book, you will find such dishes and cuisines which have the right amount of ingredients to help you make a well-balanced dish every day. Here too, there is a difference between the refined and the natural carbs. The refined carbs are bereft of any kind of natural fiber content. On the other hand, the natural carbs are wholesome nutrients that are ingested without any changes done to them.

I have come across some studies that prove refined carbs are the causative factors of an increase in diabetes in individuals.

Once you start following a strict routine with regards to your eating habits, everything will become easier. You may not like a change in your diet. But considering the fact that this change will help you lead a normal life, following it won't be difficult at all.

I get a lot of questions from patients and my family members as well. Sometimes I get calls from mothers and wives whilst they are grocery shopping to know that is a particular fruit or ingredient appropriate for diabetes or not. It can be a bit annoying at times, but then I realize why I came into this field. And that keeps me motivated to help everyone I can to make an informed choice.

When I was still in college, I stumbled upon an amazing concept of economics. It was related to asymmetric information. The theory said that until and unless, the consumer does not have the right information about the product they are about to purchase. This lack of information leads to skewness in the market perpetrated by herd behavior. That is what I want to remove with the help of my practice. I want to dissuade people from taking a wrong and ill-informed decision.

The promoters and endorsers of fad diets see this gaping void in information as an opportunity. But I am writing this book to fill that void and help you understand the reality of a diabetic diet. Also, this book will help you walk into a new lifestyle with ease.

It is not easy to adapt to a different lifestyle. But, when it comes to our health, I feel that these changes are essential for the overall development.

Apart from carbohydrates, calories also form an essential component of the daily meal. It makes me proud to say that I successfully helped a number of people to lead a healthy and satisfying life.

Satisfaction does not mean that they are not facing any kind of issues with their health. You see, diabetes can only be controlled or managed, but I have not seen people who have cured it.

Type 1 diabetes is caused by autoimmune factors. This means that the body cells attack the insulin creating cells. I have several patients coming to me and asking about why our own cells would wreak havoc inside the body. What is the reason?

Especially when the kids are suffering from this issue, it pains me even more. Because these little souls have a lot to explore and observe in their lives. And to experience the botheration and the psychological stress of suffering from such a condition is just awful.

That is why I have always wanted to promote a diet plan that will work for kids and adults alike. This immune system derived diabetes is often genetic, and its management is also a bit difficult.

It does not matter what type of diabetes you are suffering from; the key is to practice a good diet. And by good diet, I mean that you need to really maintain a balance in your diet, starting with the calories and carbohydrates.

By a balanced diet, I mean that you need to customize your meal plans as per the type of diabetes. For instance, in type 2 diabetes, some people can experience weight loss to a greater degree. And to compensate for the weight loss, they need to fulfill that requirement by taking enough calories. The real challenge to ensure that every calorie that you take is beneficial and will not add much of the sugar content. I have helped patients who earlier obese. But when they are suffering from diabetes, their body weight starts to plummet down rapidly — ultimately leading to weight loss, which is too quick and adverse to sustain that healthiness.

I have shared some of the best tips and tricks to sustain the right level of both these nutrients without compromising your overall health. This means that you will get to eat enough calories and carbs to maintain your weight and not lose out on total nutrient count.

The suggestions that you will see in the book are based on my experience, study, observation, and treating people with diabetes. I have a habit of observing everything around me. And when it comes to my profession, I keep a note of all my patients' progress and what kind of diet will suit them the best.

I have had patients for whom the rarest and unexplored ingredients work wonders, and for others, even the most promising diets do not show any result.

Preparing Diabetic Meals

This is something really fun and learning things to do. Note one thing; if you are suffering from diabetes, you need to become really selective about what you eat and from whose hands you eat it. And for the most part, your own hands are the safest ones.

It can be your mother, wife, sister, daughter, husband, son, or anyone else who can prepare meals for you. But the kind of care and acute detailing that you need in this diet will only come from your hand.

This is not to instill fear in your mind, but my motive with this book is to prepare you for a long life ahead. A life that should not necessarily be left at the pity of circumstances. I do not want you to go to a gathering and just gawk at other people's faces. But I want you to be self-sufficient and content with your diet, and you need not have to worry about what you will eat. You will find several easy to prepare and preserve dishes in the book to help you make merry in every situation.

The one and only thumb rule of a diabetic diet is that you need to start simple. By this, I mean that you will find a lot of palatable and mouth-watering dishes in the next pages. But hold your horses and go through everything first. The reason being that you need to start with easy diets and with ingredients that won't put too much pressure on your body and force adaptation.

Before we move forward, let me tell you a bit about the role of glycemic levels in diabetes. And I often get several questions from my patients, especially those who are suffering from type 2 diabetes.

Most of the time, you will have to focus on the glycemic level of the food that you will eat. Or even check for the same in the ingredients. It must be known that foods with a high glycemic level will certainly increase blood sugar levels. Contrary to it, the increase in sugar content due to lower glycemic foods will be relatively less.

The reason you will want to choose meals with a lower number of ingredients is higher than the number of ingredients more will be the glycemic levels in that dish. Hence, I have taken care to include the perfect mix of such ingredients that take care of your health and diet from all perspectives.

Smart Usage Of The Ingredients

Let me tell you, by smart, I mean reuse the everyday ingredients that you can. I get a good stare by some people when suggesting this, and others are keen to know how a person can reuse the already spent ingredients. Well, both of them have got it wrong, and I guess even you have not clearly understood what I am trying to say here.

My motive for suggesting you reuse the ingredients is to make sure that you preserve some ingredients or use them frugally. And the major motive of this reusing is to provide you with the exact flavor as the ingredient would give without adding to the total calorie count and increasing the levels of natural sugars.

For instance, there is no need to throw the lemon or orange peels. Rather, grate them and store them in the deep-freezer. The next time you want to add a lemony flavor to your dish, just add some of the stored lemons to the dish and get the same taste as you will have with using the whole lemon fruit. Isn't it amazing? Really it is. But the key here is to choose the right ingredients for reuse and also store them perfectly to sustain their taste and flavor.

Before we move forward, let me share with a real-life example of a girl who, against all the odds, tackled her diabetes problem with sheer strength and compassion. And honestly, I get a lot of patients who inspire me every day to keep on going and to keep helping people. But this girl's confidence and passion for life give me motivation in the darkest times.

I mean, as a person who has to deal with the problems of other people on a daily basis, you do, at times, want to go under the blanket and just immerse into the bed itself. Emma came to me when she was only in her sophomore year. A beautiful young girl with straight hair and amazing eyes. Her smile would seduce any man to die for her, pun intended.

Apart from her outer beauty, Emma was suffering from Type 1 diabetes from an earlier age. She did experience some symptoms early on, but her parents ignored them, and the problem aggravated. The moment Emma came to me, I knew that she was in grave trouble. Despite her difficulties, Emma was actively taking part in gymnastics and was also in the school cheerleading team. A jolly natured girl, when Emma came to know about her condition, she was in tears.

Starting out, she was a bit scared to start the diet. I somehow convinced her of the benefits of this diet and how it will help her attend college one day on the basis of her gymnastics prowess. Being a child, Emma had to face a lot of trouble. Peer pressure forced her to keep it from her friends. On the other hand, she was not allowed to eat anything from the outside, which could risk increasing the blood glucose levels in her blood.

I know that it may not sound much to you. But as a girl of such tender age and sensitivity, sharing with her friends that she is suffering from diabetes, it is easier said than done. But Emma was reluctant, and she stood the course. I helped her stay active on her diet. I would call her every day to ask about her progress. I taught her to maintain a chart and keep the daily count of her calories and carbohydrates. I had to teach her everything about the glycemic index. And she is a patient girl.

She listened to me, followed my diet plan, and in the end, Emma has become self capable of making her own dishes and even sharing them with others. Sometimes she tells me that her family and friends love Emma's cuisine better than the others. The reason being, Emma has put her years of patience, love, and care into that dish. All it takes is a little effort from your side, and everything else will fall into the right place on its own. Reading these words, you may not get juiced up enough to start this diet. But I only ask you to give it a few day's time. And once you start seeing the results, everything will become clear.

This is because you are taking a full-fledged diet and that too, with the right kind of ingredient after taking care of the daily nutritional count. The only thing that you need to identify is the right quantity of calories set per your BMI and the degree of diabetes.

As of now, there are 417 million people who are suffering from diabetes. And if we could bring them all together in one place, we could call it a diabetic country with the third-largest population in the world.

Cook Now and Rest Later

Yet another trick that you can follow is batch cooking. I have also adapted to this technique of cooking, and it really gives me a lot of time to do other things rather than spending all the time cooking.

I always recommend batch cooking for patients with diabetes. Because those who wish to prepare their own food will save a lot of time doing so. The time they will save, they can spend it either walking or doing some exercise to keep fit.

Exercising should be an essential part of your life if you are suffering from diabetes. The most important reason is that with regular exercising, the sensitivity to insulin is boosted; in turn, the blood glucose levels are increased. That is why I always recommend my patients to go for a walk in the morning. Or even exercise for at least an hour during the day.

This begs the question of how does walking or doing some pushups helps with diabetes? Well, the answer is fairly simple. You see, when a person is suffering from diabetes, there is an increased level of blood glucose in the body. This much is evident and apparent.

Insulin, which is supposed to absorb this excessive sugars, may not be working to its full capacity, something which is called Insulin Resistance in medical parlance. Other than this, it can also be due to the fact that your body is not producing insulin anymore.

Exercising or walking pumps up the muscles. They undergo rigorous contractions and expansions. This tires them, and to gain energy; they directly attack the glucose levels to acquire more amount of energy. Hence, the problem solved. Earlier, you were dependent on insulin to burn the extra glucose. Now your muscles suo moto take care of this aspect and burn the extra sugar content in your blood. It does not stop here. A Harvard study finds that exercise or walking leads to a reduction in Insulin resistance. Now tell me if there is a better and more natural solution than this to combat Diabetes.

I think I have diverted from the topic a bit. We were talking about batch cooking, right? So, when it comes to cooking collectively for the week or for the next 3 or 4 days, you will surely have more time in hand.

Finding your Rhythm

In the next part of this book, you will come across another unique aspect of tackling diabetes. Finding your rhythm means that you need to identify such a combination of the time at which you eat your meals and the time that you devote to other activities. In the end, your daily life routine should be as smooth as a shark.

No, I am not talking about the circadian rhythm that is different. What I mean to say by rhythm is that you need to find that passion. That level of interest and self-motivation where you will be able to embrace diabetes rather than fear it. I know that this may sound a bit overwhelming and superficial. But when you come to think of it, once you are found with diabetes, it is not easy or straightforward to get rid of it. Even if you take to prescription drugs that claim to cure it, until the time it will fade away, you will develop several other issues as side effects of these medicines.

I am not saying that medicines do not work. They do work, but the associated risks are much higher. Instead, if you focus on natural remedies like a healthy meal plan combined with some quintessential exercises, everything will work for the good. A good dietician will help you curate a unique diet plan that will be based on several variables. To name a few, BMI, height, weight, diabetes type, level of glucose, the viscosity of blood, body stature, and physique.

Storage Principles

I have also touched upon a number of storage principles for your food and ingredient. You need to identify the effects of storing food in the different types of containers. Some containers are BPA free others are safe to be kept in the freezer, microwaves, and whatnot.

Then there are glass containers, plastic ones, steel containers, mason jars, among others. All these different types of jars and containers are talked about in the succeeding chapters. You see, my motive is to provide you with a full-scale encyclopedia that will contain everything you need to know about the diabetic diet. Starting from the ingredient choice to how to store and preserve, you will find a massive chunk of information, which is all based on my personal experience and observation.

Other than this, I have also talked about the kitchen equipment and measuring equipment. Reiterating the fact that your meal plan has to be set in precise measurements. That is the key to a diabetic diet plan. Because your body will respond favorably to the set quantities of ingredients and plate size, keeping a strict eye on how much raw material is added to every dish is necessary.

Most of the people and not only those suffering from diabetes are riddled with something called Portion Distortion. This is what you can call the result of unregulated eating and taking the wrong amounts of food. Hence, I always recommend my patients to keep measuring cups and spoons in their kitchen. And use them while preparing every dish.

Equipment like the storage containers, food scale, digital thermometer, saucepans, cutting board, immersion blender among others, are the major weapons that should be there in your kitchen if you want to tackle diabetes successfully.

What Can You Expect From This Book?

I have already shared with you the motive of writing this book that how I want everyone suffering from diabetes to lead a healthy, informed, and well-maintained life. I do not want people like yourself or anybody else to feel left out in any circumstances. It is my personal experience, where I have seen my father suffering from health induced isolation, where he could not eat together with the family on any occasion or even go out with us for a family dinner.

I have seen several people suffer from physical and mental adversity of diabetes. It is for these individuals that I am writing this book so that they can get all the desired motivation and help.

You can expect a lot of information on how to live a lifestyle with diabetes. I tend to call it a diabetic induced lifestyle. Because when you are suffering from a disease like diabetes, everything has to change. But most importantly, your mindset has to change.

In all my years of practice, I have seen all kinds of people; some are very strong mentally that they can do anything. They have such strong will power that they can quickly adapt to this new lifestyle while others who are not so strong mentally take a lot of time to prepare themselves.

In this book, you can expect to find a bit of everything. There is a bit of motivation; there are some stories, some inspiration, scientific facts, studies, suggestions, recommendations, tips, tricks, and a lot more. This cookbook is the culmination of my years of practice as a dietician. I have gathered evidence in all these years and am sharing it all with you.

Other than this, you will be able to identify the right kind of ingredients that can be used to prepare diabetic specific dishes. Not only this, but you will also find a good number of dishes to start with, and all of them will be divided into snacks, breakfast, lunch, dinner, and salads.

The Best Meal Action Plan

Portion distortion also relates to untimely eating and unregulated eating habits. The majority of the population in developed and developing countries is at the risk of obesity. Why is that so? It is because they indulge in binge eating or dieting simultaneously. And since we are the topic, I have come across many individuals who have developed an entirely wrongful notion of dieting.

Dieting does not mean that you eat as much as you can, and then for the next month, you do not eat food. In this scenario, we are confusing our bodies. Whenever you eat food in a set rhythm and continue the same pattern continuously, your body is so smart that it will automatically adapt to it. And when you change the pattern, it will show what we can call withdrawal symptoms.

Withdrawal symptoms are not just limited to drugs. It can be related to anything. The basic understanding is that you are altering the set routine to which your body had earlier was adjusted. And when you change it, the effects that show themselves are called withdrawal symptoms.

That is why I never recommend unplanned dieting. If you want to go for dieting, irrespective of the kind, degree, and type of diet, always ease into it. Start slow, and gradually, you need to progress to higher degrees of eating habits.

To this end, what you will find in this book are some additional tips and tricks that will help you undergo a smooth transition. The diabetic diet is like entering a portal from one end and coming out of the next. The journey between these two portals that is what this book is all about.

Using this book is as easy as it gets. In the first chapters, you will get to a lot about calories and carbohydrates, which plays a significant role in deciding how your diet plan will be framed. You will come to know the right amount of calories and carbohydrates required for every individual depending on several variables. Added to this, you will learn to compartmentalize your plate into set proportions of starch, carbohydrates, and calories.

There are a lot of things that you will have to change. Don't be alarmed. I know that change is not easy for everyone, but it is inevitable. So it is better to conform with it rather than going against it and facing more troubles.

Finally, before you move on to the next chapters, hear that this book helps me to realize my lifelong dream of assisting people in dealing with diabetes confidently. I consider it my bounden duty to help you understand that there is no difference between a diabetic and a normal diet. Instead, I would say that eating a regular diet without any supervision is only a disaster waiting to happen. Even if you are not suffering from diabetes, eat right and eat good, because in the end, what you eat is what you will become.

Breakfast Recipes

Herb & Vegetable Egg White Omelet 12
Lemon Chia Parfait with Berries 13
Whole Wheat Banana Cinnamon Pancakes 14
Denver Omelet Breakfast Salad 15
Fruit and Nut Granola 16
Easy Egg Scramble 17
Spiced Overnight Oats 18
Eggs Baked in Peppers 19
Spinach and Ham Egg Muffins 20
Banana Matcha Breakfast Smoothie 21
Cinnamon Oat Pancakes 22
Easy Vegetable Frittata 23
Vanilla Mixed Berry Smoothie 24

Herb & Vegetable Egg White Omelet

Prep Time: 10 minutes
Cook Time: 10 minutes
Servings: 1

Ingredients:
- 1/4 cup diced red pepper
- 1/4 cup diced tomatoes
- 1/4 cup diced red onion
- 4 large egg whites
- Salt and pepper
- 1 teaspoon fresh chopped basil
- 1 teaspoon fresh chopped parsley

Nutrition Facts Per Serving:
Calories 100, Total Fat 0.4g, Saturated Fat 0g, Total Carbs 7.8g, Net Carbs 6.2g, Protein 15.5g, Sugar 4.9g, Fiber 1.6g, Sodium 138mg

Instructions:
1. Heat a medium non-stick skillet over medium heat and grease with cooking spray.

2. Add the peppers, tomatoes, and onions to the skillet.

3. Season with salt and pepper and sauté for 4 to 5 minutes until tender.

4. Spoon the veggies off into a bowl and reheat the skillet with more cooking spray.

5. Whisk the egg whites with a little salt and pepper then pour into the skillet.

6. Cook for 1 minute without disturbing then tilt the pan to spread the uncooked egg.

7. Let the egg cook until the edges start to set then spoon the veggies over half.

8. Sprinkle with the basil and parsley then fold the egg over the toppings.

9. Cook until the egg is set then slide onto a plate to serve.

Lemon Chia Parfait with Berries

Prep Time: 15 minutes
Cook Time: None
Servings: 4

Ingredients:
- 2 cups low-fat Greek yogurt, plain
- 2 tablespoons fresh lemon juice
- 1 tablespoon fresh lemon zest
- 1 teaspoon liquid stevia extract
- 2 tablespoons chia seeds
- 1 cup fresh blueberries
- 1 cup fresh diced strawberries

Nutrition Facts Per Serving:
Calories 140, Total Fat 2.8g, Saturated Fat 0.3g, Total Carbs 16.4g, Net Carbs 12.2g, Protein 15.1g, Sugar 10.5g, Fiber 4.2g, Sodium 64mg

Instructions:
1. Spoon the yogurt into a medium mixing bowl.
2. Stir in the lemon juice, lemon zest, and liquid stevia extract.
3. Add the chia seeds and vanilla extract then stir well.
4. Let rest for 5 minutes until the yogurt is thickened.
5. Spoon one-third the yogurt mixture into four parfait glasses.
6. Divide half the berries among the parfait glasses.
7. Add another layer of yogurt and berries to each glass and chill until ready to eat.

Whole Wheat Banana Cinnamon Pancakes

Prep Time: 10 minutes
Cook Time: 15 minutes
Servings: 8

Ingredients:
- 1 cup whole-wheat flour
- 1 cup white flour
- 4 teaspoons baking powder
- 1 1/2 teaspoons ground cinnamon
- 1/2 teaspoon salt
- 2 cups fat-free milk
- 2 large eggs, whisked
- 1 tablespoon canola oil
- 1/2 teaspoon vanilla extract
- 1/4 teaspoon liquid stevia extract
- 1 medium banana, mashed

Nutrition Facts Per Serving:
Calories 205, Total Fat 3.4g, Saturated Fat 0.6g, Total Carbs 35.5g, Net Carbs 33.9g, Protein 7.5g, Sugar 5g, Fiber 1.6g, Sodium 200mg

Instructions:

1. Whisk together the whole wheat flour, white flour, baking powder, cinnamon, and salt in a medium mixing bowl.

2. In a separate bowl, whisk together the milk, eggs, oil, vanilla, and stevia extract.

3. Stir the wet ingredients into the dry and fold in the mashed banana until just combined.

4. Preheat an electric griddle or a large nonstick skillet over medium heat.

5. Spoon the batter onto the pan 1/4 cup at a time and cook until bubbles form in the surface of the batter.

6. Carefully flip the pancakes and cook until browned underneath.

7. Transfer the pancakes to a plate and keep warm while you repeat with remaining batter.

8. Store the leftover pancakes in the fridge or freezer and reheat in the oven at 375° F for 10 to 15 minutes.

Denver Omelet Breakfast Salad

Prep Time: 10 minutes
Cook Time: 15 minutes
Servings: 1

Ingredients:
- 2 cups fresh baby spinach
- 1/4 cup fresh chopped tomatoes
- 2 tablespoons diced red onion
- 1 teaspoon olive oil
- 1/2 cup diced fat-free ham
- 1/4 cup diced green pepper
- 2 large eggs
- Salt and pepper

Nutrition Facts Per Serving:
Calories 320, Total Fat 18.9g, Saturated Fat 5.1g, Total Carbs 8.8g, Net Carbs 6.1g, Protein 29.8g, Sugar 3.6g, Fiber 2.7g, Sodium 1033mg

Instructions:

1. Toss the spinach, tomatoes, and red onion together on a salad plate – set aside.

2. Heat the oil in a medium skillet over medium-high heat.

3. Add the ham and green pepper then sauté for 6 to 7 minutes.

4. Spoon the cooked ham and peppers onto the salad.

5. Reheat the skillet and crack two eggs into it – season with salt and pepper.

6. Cook the eggs to your liking and spoon over the salad to serve.

Fruit and Nut Granola

Prep Time: 10 minutes
Cook Time: 20 minutes
Servings: 9

Ingredients:
- 2 1/2cups old-fashioned oats
- 1/2 cup sliced almonds
- 1/4 cup sunflower seeds
- 1/4 cup whole flaxseed
- 1/4 cup honey
- 1 tablespoon canola oil
- 1 teaspoon vanilla extract
- 1/2 teaspoon ground cinnamon
- 1/4 teaspoon salt
- 1/2 cup dried cranberries (unsweetened)
- 1/4 cup dried banana chips

Nutrition Facts Per Serving: (1/2 cup)
Calories 185, Total Fat 10g, Saturated Fat 1.5g, Total Carbs 22.7g, Net Carbs 17.7g, Protein 4.8g, Sugar 8.9g, Fiber 5g, Sodium 69mg

Instructions:
1. Combine the oats, almonds, sunflower seeds, and flaxseed in a large bowl and toss well to combine.

2. Warm the honey and canola oil in the microwave until thin.

3. Stir in the vanilla, ground cinnamon, and salt.

4. Drizzle the mixture over the dry ingredients and toss well to combine.

5. Toss in the cranberries and banana chips.

6. Spread the mixture onto a parchment-lined baking sheet.

7. Bake at 350° F for 20 minutes until browned, stirring every 5 to 8 minutes.

8. Cool completely on a wire rack then break up into pieces and store in an airtight container. Serve with fat-free milk, if desired.

Easy Egg Scramble

Prep Time: 5 minutes
Cook Time: 10 minutes
Servings: 1

Ingredients:
- 2 large eggs
- 1 tablespoon fat-free milk
- Salt and pepper
- 1/4 cup diced green pepper
- 2 tablespoons diced onion
- 1/4 cup diced tomatoes

Nutrition Facts Per Serving:
Calories 170, Total Fat 10.1g, Saturated Fat 3.1g, Total Carbs 6.3g, Net Carbs 4.9g, Protein 13.9g, Sugar 4.1g, Fiber 1.4g, Sodium 152mg

Instructions:

1. Whisk together the eggs, milk, salt, and pepper in a small bowl.

2. Heat a medium skillet over medium-high heat and grease with cooking spray.

3. Add the green pepper and onion then cook for 2 to 3 minutes.

4. Spoon the veggies into a bowl then reheat the skillet.

5. Pour in the egg mixture and cook until the eggs start to thicken.

6. Spoon in the cooked veggies and diced tomatoes.

7. Stir the mixture and cook until the egg is set and scrambled. Serve hot.

Spiced Overnight Oats

Prep Time: 10 minutes
Cook Time: None
Servings: 6

Ingredients:
- 2 cups old-fashioned oats
- 1 cup fat-free milk
- 1 tablespoon vanilla extract
- 1 teaspoon liquid stevia extract
- 1 teaspoon ground cinnamon
- 1/4 teaspoon ground nutmeg
- 1/2 cup toasted walnuts, chopped

Nutrition Facts Per Serving:
Calories 140, Total Fat 7.1g, Saturated Fat 0.5g, Total Carbs 12.7g, Net Carbs 10.4g, Protein 5.6g, Sugar 2.6g, Fiber 2.3g, Sodium 23mg

Instructions:

1. Stir together the oats, milk, vanilla extract, liquid stevia extract, cinnamon, and nutmeg in a large bowl.

2. Cover and chill overnight until thick.

3. Stir in the yogurt just before serving and spoon into cups.

4. Top with chopped walnuts and fresh fruit to serve.

Eggs Baked in Peppers

Prep Time: 5 minutes
Cook Time: 25 minutes
Servings: 4

Ingredients:
- 4 medium bell peppers, assorted
- 1 cup shredded low-fat cheddar cheese
- 8 large eggs
- Salt and pepper
- Fresh chopped parsley, to serve

Nutrition Facts Per Serving:
Calories 260, Total Fat 16.3g, Saturated Fat 6.6g, Total Carbs 10.9g, Net Carbs 9.3g, Protein 20.8g, Sugar 6.8g, Fiber 1.6g, Sodium 374mg

Instructions:
1. Preheat the oven to 400°F and slice the peppers in half.
2. Remove the seeds and pith from each pepper and place them cut-side up in a baking dish large enough to fit them all.
3. Divide the shredded cheese among the pepper halves and crack an egg into each.
4. Season with salt and pepper then bake for 20 to 25 minutes until done to your liking.
5. Garnish with fresh chopped parsley to serve.

Spinach and Ham Egg Muffins

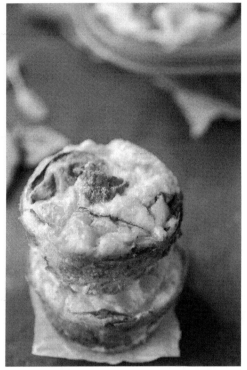

Prep Time: 10 minutes
Cook Time: 20 minutes
Servings: 6 (2-pieces)

Ingredients:
- 6 large eggs
- 1/2 cup fat-free milk
- Salt and pepper
- 5 ounces fresh baby spinach, chopped
- 1 cup diced fat-free ham
- 1/2 cup diced red pepper
- 1/2 cup shredded mozzarella cheese, part-skim

Nutrition Facts Per Serving:
Calories 130, Total Fat 6.8g, Saturated Fat 2.2g, Total Carbs 3.4g, Net Carbs 0.7g, Protein 13.3g, Sugar 2g, Fiber 0.7g, Sodium 395mg

Instructions:

1. Preheat the oven to 350° F and grease a 12-cup muffin pan with cooking spray.

2. Beat together the eggs, milk, salt, and pepper in a medium bowl.

3. Stir in the spinach, ham, and peppers then spoon into the muffin cups.

4. Sprinkle with cheese and bake for 20 minutes or until the egg is set.

5. Cool for 5 minutes then remove and serve warm.

Banana Matcha Breakfast Smoothie

Prep Time: 5 minutes
Cook Time: None
Servings: 1

Ingredients:
- 1 cup fat-free milk
- 1 medium banana, sliced
- 1/4 cup frozen chopped pineapple
- 1/2 cup ice cubes
- 1 tablespoon matcha powder
- 1/4 teaspoon ground cinnamon
- Liquid stevia extract, to taste

Nutrition Facts Per Serving:
Calories 230, Total Fat 0.4g, Saturated Fat 0.1g, Total Carbs 44.9g, Net Carbs 38g, Protein 12.6g, Sugar 30.9g, Fiber 6.9g, Sodium 135mg

Instructions:

1. Combine the ingredients in a blender.

2. Pulse the mixture several times to chop the ingredients.

3. Blend for 30 to 60 seconds until smooth and well combined.

4. Sweeten to taste with liquid stevia extract, if desired.

5. Pour into a glass and serve immediately.

Cinnamon Oat Pancakes

Prep Time: 10 minutes
Cook Time: 15 minutes
Servings: 6

Ingredients:
- 1 cup old-fashioned oats
- 1 cup whole-wheat flour
- 2 teaspoons baking powder
- 1 teaspoon salt
- 1 1/2 cups fat-free milk
- 1/4 cup canola oil
- 2 large eggs, whisked
- 1 teaspoon lemon juice
- 1/2 to 1 teaspoon liquid stevia extract

Nutrition Facts Per Serving:
Calories 230, Total Fat 11.4g, Saturated Fat 1.3g, Total Carbs 24.3g, Net Carbs 23g, Protein 7.1g, Sugar 3.3g, Fiber 1.3g, Sodium 446mg

Instructions:

1. Combine the oats, flour, baking powder, and salt in a medium mixing bowl.

2. In a separate bowl, stir together the milk, canola oil, eggs, lemon juice, and stevia extract.

3. Stir the wet ingredients into the dry until just combined.

4. Heat a large skillet or griddle to medium-high heat and grease with cooking spray.

5. Spoon the batter in 1/4 cups into the skillet and cook until bubbles form on the surface.

6. Flip the pancakes and cook to brown on the other side.

7. Slide onto a plate and repeat with the remaining batter.

8. Store the extra pancakes in an airtight container and reheat in the microwave or oven.

Easy Vegetable Frittata

Prep Time: 5 minutes
Cook Time: 25 minutes
Servings: 4

Ingredients:
- 8 large eggs
- 1/3 cup fat-free milk
- Salt and pepper
- 2 tablespoons olive oil
- 1 medium red pepper, diced
- 1/3 cup diced yellow onion
- 2 cups fresh baby spinach
- 4 ounces feta cheese, crumbled

Nutrition Facts Per Serving:
Calories 305, Total Fat 23.1g, Saturated Fat 8.4g, Total Carbs 7.1g, Net Carbs 6g, Protein 18.2g, Sugar 5.1g, Fiber 1.1g, Sodium 480mg

Instructions:
1. Preheat the oven to 350° F.
2. Whisk together the eggs, milk, salt, and pepper then set aside.
3. Heat the oil in a medium oven-proof skillet over medium heat.
4. Add the red pepper and onion and sauté for 5 minutes.
5. Stir in the spinach and cook 2 minutes more until wilted.
6. Spread the veggies in the skillet and crumble the cheese over top.
7. Pour in the egg and cook until the edges start to set, about 2 minutes.
8. Transfer to the oven and bake for 15 minutes or until the egg is cooked through.
9. Cool for 5 minutes before slicing to serve.

Vanilla Mixed Berry Smoothie

Prep Time: 5 minutes
Cook Time: None
Servings: 1

Ingredients:
- 1 cup fat-free milk
- 1/2 cup nonfat Greek yogurt, plain
- 1/2 cup frozen blueberries
- 1/4 cup frozen strawberries
- 3 to 4 ice cubes
- 1 teaspoon fresh lemon juice
- Liquid stevia extract, to taste

Nutrition Facts Per Serving:
Calories 220, Total Fat 0.3g, Saturated Fat 0g, Total Carbs 31.6g, Net Carbs 28.3g, Protein 21.6g, Sugar 27.3g, Fiber 3.3g, Sodium 204mg

Instructions:

1. Combine the ingredients in a blender.

2. Pulse the mixture several times to chop the ingredients.

3. Blend for 30 to 60 seconds until smooth and well combined.

4. Sweeten to taste with liquid stevia extract, if desired.

5. Pour into a glass and serve immediately.

Lunch Recipes

Asian Crab Noodle Salad 26
Chicken Tortilla Soup 27
Turkey & Brown Rice Lettuce Cups 28
Shrimp and Black Bean Salad 29
Chicken, Spinach, and Pesto Soup 30
Creamy Broccoli Chickpea Salad 31
Chickpea, Tuna, and Kale Salad 32
Avocado Veggie Wrap 33
Grilled Avocado Hummus Paninis 34
Ceviche-Stuffed Avocado Halves 35
Carrot Ginger Soup 36
Avocado White Bean Sandwich 37
Turkey Cobb Salad 38

Asian Cold Noodle Salad

Prep Time: 15 minutes
Cook Time: None
Servings: 1

Ingredients:
- 3 tablespoons light coconut milk
- 2 tablespoons whipped peanut butter
- 1 tablespoon water
- 1 tablespoon fresh lime juice
- 1/2 tablespoon soy sauce
- 1/4 to 1/2 teaspoon sriracha sauce
- 1 ounce whole-wheat spaghetti, cooked
- 1/2 cup snow peas, halved
- 2 ounces cooked chicken breast, chopped
- 1/4 cup diced red pepper
- 1 teaspoon fresh chopped cilantro
- 1 green onion, sliced thin

Nutrition Facts Per Serving:
Calories 375, Total Fat 15g, Saturated Fat 3.1g, Total Carbs 36.3g, Net Carbs 28.2g, Protein 26.2g, Sugar 8.3g, Fiber 8.1g, Sodium 627mg

Instructions:

1. Stir together the coconut milk, peanut butter, water, lime juice, soy sauce, and sriracha sauce in a small bowl.

2. Cook the spaghetti to al dente then drain and rinse under cool water.

3. Combine the cooled spaghetti, snow peas, chicken, red pepper, and cilantro in a bowl.

4. Toss with the dressing until well coated then serve with sliced green onion.

Chicken Tortilla Soup

Prep Time: 10 minutes
Cook Time: 20 minutes
Servings: 6

Ingredients:
- 1 tablespoon olive oil
- 1/2 small yellow onion, diced
- 3 cloves minced garlic
- 2 cups fat-free chicken broth
- 1 (15-ounce) can black beans, rinsed and drained
- 1 cup crushed tomatoes
- 2 tablespoons tomato paste
- 1 teaspoon ground cumin
- 1/2 teaspoon paprika
- Salt and pepper
- 8 ounces cooked chicken breast, shredded
- 1 tablespoon fresh lime juice
- 1 tablespoon fresh chopped cilantro
- 1 medium diced avocado, optional

Nutrition Facts Per Serving:
Calories 410, Total Fat 11g, Saturated Fat 2g, Total Carbs 52.8g, Net Carbs 38g, Protein 27.5g, Sugar 5g, Fiber 14.8g, Sodium 241mg

Instructions:

1. Heat the oil in a large saucepan over medium heat.

2. Add the onion and sauté for 3 minutes then stir in the garlic and cook 1 minute more.

3. Pour in the chicken broth, beans, tomatoes, tomato paste, cumin, and paprika.

4. Bring to a light boil then simmer for 10 minutes.

5. Season with salt and pepper then stir in the cooked chicken.

6. Cook until the chicken is heated through then remove from heat.

7. Stir in the lime juice and cilantro then adjust seasoning to taste.

8. Serve hot with diced avocado.

Turkey & Brown Rice Lettuce Cups

Prep Time: 10 minutes
Cook Time: 15 minutes
Servings: 4

Ingredients:
- 1/2 cup water
- 1/2 cup instant brown rice
- 1 tablespoon sesame oil
- 1 pound 93% lean ground turkey
- 1 tablespoon fresh grated ginger
- 1 medium red pepper, diced
- 1/2 cup fat-free chicken broth
- 1 1/2 tablespoons soy sauce
- 1 teaspoon Chinese 5-spice powder
- Salt to taste
- 2 heads Boston lettuce, leaves separated
- Shredded carrot, to serve
- Fresh cilantro, to serve

Nutrition Facts Per Serving:
Calories 270, Total Fat 12.1g, Saturated Fat 3g, Total Carbs 14.7g, Net Carbs 12.3g, Protein 24g, Sugar 4.1g, Fiber 2.4g, Sodium 529mg

Instructions:

1. Bring the water to boil in a small saucepan then stir in the rice.

2. Reduce heat to low and cook, covered, for 5 minutes then set aside off the heat.

3. Heat the oil in a large skillet over medium-high heat and add the turkey and ginger.

4. Cook for 5 minutes, crumbling the turkey with a spoon.

5. Stir in the cooked rice along with the peppers, broth, soy sauce, spices, and salt.

6. Cook for 1 minute until heated through.

7. Spoon the turkey and brown rice mixture into lettuce cups.

8. Garnish with shredded carrot and cilantro to serve.

Shrimp and Black Bean Salad

Prep Time: 10 minutes
Cook Time: None
Servings: 6

Ingredients:
- 1/4 cup apple cider vinegar
- 3 tablespoons olive oil
- 1 teaspoon ground cumin
- 1/4 teaspoon chipotle chili powder
- 1/2 teaspoon salt
- 1 pound cooked shrimp, peeled and deveined
- 1 (15-ounce) can black beans, rinsed and drained
- 1 cup diced tomatoes
- 1 small green pepper, diced
- 1/4 cup sliced green onions
- 1/4 cup fresh chopped cilantro

Nutrition Facts Per Serving:
Calories 405, Total Fat 9.5g, Saturated Fat 1.7g, Total Carbs 47.8g, Net Carbs 36.2, Protein 33.1, Sugar 2.8g, Fiber 11.6g, Sodium 291mg

Instructions:

1. Whisk together the vinegar, olive oil, cumin, chili powder, and salt in a large bowl.

2. Chop the shrimp into bite-sized pieces then add to the bowl.

3. Toss in the beans, tomatoes, bell pepper, green onion, and cilantro until well combined.

4. Cover and chill until ready to serve.

Chicken, Spinach, and Pesto Soup

Prep Time: 10 minutes
Cook Time: 15 minutes
Servings: 6

Ingredients:

- 1 tablespoon olive oil
- 1 small red pepper, diced
- 10 ounces boneless, skinless chicken breast
- 1 clove minced garlic
- 5 1/2 cups fat-free chicken broth
- 1 1/2 teaspoons dried basil
- 6 ounces fresh baby spinach, chopped
- 1 (15-ounce) white cannellini beans, rinsed and drained
- 2 tablespoons basil pesto
- Salt and pepper

Nutrition Facts Per Serving:

Calories 190, Total Fat 13g, Saturated Fat 2g, Total Carbs 10g, Net Carbs 6.1g, Protein 19.7g, Sugar 1.4g, Fiber 3.9g, Sodium 460mg

Instructions:

1. Heat the oil in a large saucepan over medium-high heat.

2. Add the red pepper and chicken then sauté for 4 minutes until the chicken is browned.

3. Stir in the garlic and cook for 1 minute more.

4. Add the chicken broth and dried basil then bring to a boil.

5. Reduce heat and simmer for 5 minutes until the chicken is cooked through.

6. Remove the chicken to a cutting board and chop it.

7. Add the spinach and beans to the soup and return to a gentle boil.

8. Simmer for 5 minutes then add the chicken back to the pot.

9. Stir in the pesto then season with salt and pepper to taste and serve hot.

Creamy Broccoli Chickpea Salad

Prep Time: 15 minutes
Cook Time: 2 minutes
Servings: 4

Ingredients:
- 3 cups diced broccoli
- 1/4 cup nonfat Greek yogurt, plain
- 1 tablespoon fresh lemon juice
- 1 clove minced garlic
- 1/4 teaspoon fresh ground pepper
- 1 (7-ounce) can chickpeas, rinsed and drained
- 1/2 cup diced red pepper
- 1/4 cup crumbled feta cheese

Nutrition Facts Per Serving:
Calories 240, Total Fat 5.3g, Saturated Fat 1.7g, Total Carbs 37g, Net Carbs 26.3g, Protein 14.2g, Sugar 8.2g, Fiber 10.7g, Sodium 147mg

Instructions:

1. Bring a medium pot of water to boil then add the broccoli.

2. Blanch the broccoli for 60 to 90 seconds then immediately drain and rinse in cool water.

3. Whisk together the yogurt, lemon juice, garlic, and pepper in a medium bowl.

4. Toss in the broccoli, chickpeas, red pepper, and feta cheese.

5. Season with salt and pepper to taste and serve chilled.

Chickpea, Tuna, and Kale Salad

Prep Time: 10 minutes
Cook Time: None
Servings: 1

Ingredients:
- 2 ounces fresh kale
- 2 tablespoons fat-free honey mustard dressing
- 1 (3-ounce) pouch tuna in water, drained
- 1 medium carrot, shredded
- Salt and pepper

Nutrition Facts Per Serving:
Calories 215, Total Fat 0.6g, Saturated Fat 0g, Total Carbs 28.1g, Net Carbs 23.6g, Protein 22.5g, Sugar 16g, Fiber 4.5g, Sodium 1176mg

Instructions:
1. Trim the thick stems from the kale and cut into bite-sized pieces.
2. Toss the kale with the dressing in a salad bowl.
3. Top with tuna, chickpeas, and carrots. Season with salt and pepper to serve.

Avocado Veggie Wrap

Prep Time: 15 minutes
Cook Time: None
Servings: 1

Ingredients:
- 1 low-carb multigrain wrap
- 1/4 medium avocado, peeled and chopped
- 1/4 teaspoon fresh lime juice
- 1 medium carrot, shredded
- 1/4 cup diced cucumber
- 1/4 cup diced red pepper
- 1 tablespoon crumbled feta cheese

Nutrition Facts Per Serving:
Calories 225, Total Fat 13.9g, Saturated Fat 3.5g, Total Carbs 24.9g, Net Carbs 12.5g, Protein 9.3g, Sugar 5.6g, Fiber 12.4g, Sodium 251mg

Instructions:

1. Lay the wrap out on a flat surface or a plate.

2. Mash the avocado with the lime juice in a small bowl then spread over the wrap.

3. Add the carrot, cucumber, and red pepper down the middle of the wrap.

4. Sprinkle with feta cheese then fold in the sides.

5. Roll the wrap up around the fillings and slice in half to enjoy.

Grilled Avocado Hummus Paninis

Prep Time: 15 minutes
Cook Time: 10 minutes
Servings: 4

Ingredients:
- 4 whole-wheat sandwich thins, split in half
- 1/3 cup roasted red pepper hummus
- 1/2 medium avocado, pitted and sliced thin
- Fresh ground pepper
- 1 cup fresh baby spinach, chopped
- 2 ounces feta cheese

Nutrition Facts Per Serving:
Calories 230, Total Fat 11.2g, Saturated Fat 3.2g, Total Carbs 27.8g, Net Carbs 19.2g, Protein 8.5g, Sugar 3.5g, Fiber 8.6g, Sodium 508mg

Instructions:

1. Lay the sandwich thins out flat.

2. Spread the hummus evenly on both sides of each sandwich thin.

3. Layer the avocado slices on the bottom of each sandwich thin and season with fresh ground black pepper.

4. Top each sandwich with 1/4 cup spinach and 1/2 ounce cheese.

5. Add the top to each sandwich and press down lightly.

6. Grease a large skillet with cooking spray and heat over medium heat.

7. Add one or two sandwiches and place a heavy skillet on top.

8. Cook for 2 minutes or until the bottoms are toasted.

9. Flip the sandwiches and repeat on the other side. Cut in half to serve.

Ceviche-Stuffed Avocado Halves

Prep Time: 30 minutes
Cook Time: None
Servings: 6

Ingredients:
- 2 lemons, juiced
- 2 limes, juiced
- 3 to 4 drops liquid stevia extract
- 6 ounces cooked shrimp, chopped
- 1/4 cup diced seedless cucumber
- 1/4 cup diced tomato
- 1 jalapeno, seeded and minced (optional)
- 2 tablespoons fresh chopped cilantro
- 1 tablespoon olive oil
- Salt
- 3 medium avocados

Instructions:
1. Whisk together the lemon juice, lime juice, and liquid stevia in a medium bowl.
2. Toss in the shrimp then cover and chill for 20 minutes.
3. Drain the shrimp and toss with the cucumber, tomato, jalapeno, and cilantro.
4. Drizzle with olive oil then season with salt and toss well to combine.
5. Cut the avocados in half and remove the pits.
6. Spoon 1/4 cup of the shrimp mixture onto each half to serve.

Nutrition Facts Per Serving:
Calories 270, Total Fat 22.6g, Saturated Fat 4.7g, Total Carbs 11.2g, Net Carbs 4.1g, Protein 8.7g, Sugar 1.4g, Fiber 7.1g, Sodium 106mg

Carrot Ginger Soup

Prep Time: 10 minutes
Cook Time: 20 minutes
Servings: 4

Ingredients:
- 1 tablespoon olive oil
- 1 medium yellow onion, chopped
- 3 cups fat-free chicken broth
- 1 pound carrots, peeled and chopped
- 1 tablespoon fresh grated ginger
- 1/4 cup fat-free sour cream
- Salt and pepper

Nutrition Facts Per Serving:
Calories 125, Total Fat 3.6g, Saturated Fat 0.5g, Total Carbs 17.2g, Net Carbs 13.6g, Protein 6.4g, Sugar 7.8g, Fiber 3.6g, Sodium 385mg

Instructions:
1. Heat the oil in a large saucepan over medium heat.
2. Add the onions and sauté for 5 minutes until softened.
3. Stir in the broth, carrots, and ginger then cover and bring to a boil
4. Reduce heat and simmer for 20 minutes.
5. Stir in the sour cream then remove from heat.
6. Blend using an immersion blender until smooth and creamy.
7. Season with salt and pepper to taste then serve hot.

Avocado White Bean Sandwich

Prep Time: 15 minutes
Cook Time: None
Servings: 8

Ingredients:
- 2 medium avocado, pitted and chopped
- 1 (15-ounce) can white beans, rinsed and drained
- 2 tablespoons fresh lemon juice
- 1 tablespoon olive oil
- 1 to 2 cloves minced garlic
- Salt and pepper
- 8 slices whole-wheat or whole-grain bread
- 4 slices low-fat cheddar cheese
- 4 leaves romaine lettuce, halved

Instructions:

1. Combine the avocado, white beans, lemon juice, olive oil, and garlic in a medium bowl.

2. Mash the ingredients together with a fork then season with salt and pepper to taste.

3. Toast the slices of bread to your liking.

4. Spread the avocado white bean mixture on the slices of toast.

5. Top each with a half slice of cheese and a lettuce leaf to serve.

Nutrition Facts Per Serving:
Calories 390, Total Fat 14.1g, Saturated Fat 3.3g, Total Carbs 48.2g, Net Carbs 34.8g, Protein 20.3g, Sugar 3.2g, Fiber 13.4g, Sodium 207mg

Turkey Cobb Salad

Prep Time: 15 minutes
Cook Time: None
Servings: 4

Ingredients:
- 3 tablespoons red wine vinegar
- 3 tablespoons olive oil
- 1 tablespoon Dijon mustard
- Salt and pepper
- 8 cups fresh chopped romaine
- 1/4 cup thinly sliced red onion
- 1 cup diced tomatoes
- 1 cup diced cucumber
- 4 ounces smoked turkey, sliced
- 4 slices turkey bacon, cooked and chopped
- 4 large hardboiled eggs, peeled and sliced

Nutrition Facts Per Serving:
Calories 235, Total Fat 16.8g, Saturated Fat 3.1g, Total Carbs 5g, Net Carbs 4g, Protein 15.3g, Sugar 3g, Fiber 1g, Sodium 459mg

Instructions:

1. Whisk together the vinegar, olive oil, mustard, salt, and pepper in a small bowl.

2. Divide the lettuce, red onion, tomatoes, and cucumber among four salad plates.

3. Top each with 1/4 of the turkey and turkey bacon.

4. Add a sliced egg to each salad and drizzle with dressing to serve.

Dinner Recipes

Almond-Crusted Salmon 40
Chicken & Veggie Bowl with Brown Rice 41
Beef Fajitas 42
Sautéed Turkey Bowl 43
Chicken Mushroom Stroganoff 44
Grilled Tuna Kebabs 45
Cast-Iron Pork Loin 46
Crispy Baked Tofu 47
Tilapia with Coconut Rice 48
Spicy Turkey Tacos 49
Quick and Easy Shrimp Stir-Fry 50
Chicken Burrito Bowl with Quinoa 51
Baked Salmon Cakes 52

Almond-Crusted Salmon

Prep Time: 10 minutes
Cook Time: 15 minutes
Servings: 4

Ingredients:
- 1/4 cup almond meal
- 1/4 cup whole-wheat breadcrumbs
- 1/4 teaspoon ground coriander
- 1/8 teaspoon ground cumin
- 4 (6-ounce) boneless salmon fillets
- 1 tablespoon fresh lemon juice
- Salt and pepper

Nutrition Facts Per Serving:
Calories 295, Total Fat 14.3g, Saturated Fat 1.9g, Total Carbs 6.5g, Net Carbs 5.4g, Protein 35.5g, Sugar 0.5g, Fiber 1.1g, Sodium 128mg

Instructions:
1. Preheat the oven to 500° F and line a small baking dish with foil.
2. Combine the almond meal, breadcrumbs, coriander, and cumin in a small bowl.
3. Rinse the fish in cool water then pat dry and brush with lemon juice.
4. Season the fish with salt and pepper then dredge in the almond mixture on both sides.
5. Place the fish in the baking dish and bake for 15 minutes until it just flakes with a fork.

Chicken & Veggie Bowl with Brown Rice

Prep Time: 10 minutes
Cook Time: 20 minutes
Servings: 4

Ingredients:
- 1 cup instant brown rice
- 1/4 cup tahini
- 1/4 cup fresh lemon juice
- 2 cloves minced garlic
- 1/4 teaspoon ground cumin
- Pinch salt
- 1 tablespoon olive oil
- 4 (4-ounce) chicken breast halves
- 1/2 medium yellow onion, sliced
- 1 cup green beans, trimmed
- 1 cup chopped broccoli
- 4 cups chopped kale

Nutrition Facts Per Serving:
Calories 435, Total Fat 20.5g, Saturated Fat 4.1g, Total Carbs 24.1g, Net Carbs 19.3g, Protein 39.9g, Sugar 1.8g, Fiber 4.8g, Sodium 196mg

Instructions:
1. Bring 1 cup water to boil in a small saucepan.
2. Stir in the brown rice and simmer for 5 minutes then cover and set aside.
3. Meanwhile, whisk together the tahini with 1/4 cup water in a small bowl.
4. Stir in the lemon juice, garlic, and cumin with a pinch of salt and stir well.
5. Heat the oil in a large cast-iron skillet over medium heat.
6. Season the chicken with salt and pepper then add to the skillet.
7. Cook for 3 to 5 minutes on each side until cooked through then remove to a cutting board and cover loosely with foil.
8. Reheat the skillet and cook the onion for 2 minutes then stir in the broccoli and beans.
9. Sauté for 2 minutes then stir in the kale and sauté 2 minutes more.
10. Add 2 tablespoons of water then cover and steam for 2 minutes while you slice the chicken.
11. Build the bowls with brown rice, sliced chicken, and sautéed veggies.
12. Serve hot drizzled with the lemon tahini dressing.

Beef Fajitas

Prep Time: 10 minutes
Cook Time: 15 minutes
Servings: 4

Ingredients:
- 1 lbs. lean beef sirloin, sliced thin
- 1 tablespoon olive oil
- 1 medium red onion, sliced
- 1 red pepper, sliced thin
- 1 green pepper, sliced thin
- 1/2 teaspoon ground cumin
- 1/2 teaspoon chili powder
- 8 (6-inch) whole-wheat tortillas
- Fat-free sour cream

Nutrition Facts Per Serving:
Calories 430, Total Fat 14.8g, Saturated Fat 3.2g, Total Carbs 30.5g, Net Carbs 12.9g, Protein 41.2g, Sugar 3.4g, Fiber 17.6g, Sodium 561mg

Instructions:

1. Heat a large cast-iron skillet over medium heat then add the oil.

2. Add the sliced beef and cook in a single layer for 1 minute on each side.

3. Remove the beef to a bowl and cover to keep warm.

4. Reheat the skillet then add the onions and peppers – season with cumin and chili powder.

5. Stir-fry the veggies to your liking then add to the bowl with the beef.

6. Serve hot in small whole-wheat tortillas with sliced avocado and fat-free sour cream.

Sautéed Turkey Bowl

Prep Time: 20 minutes
Cook Time: 10 minutes
Servings: 1

Ingredients:
- 4 ounces boneless, skinless turkey breast
- 1 teaspoon olive oil
- 1 1/2 teaspoons balsamic vinegar
- 1/2 teaspoon dried basil
- 1/4 teaspoon dried thyme
- Salt and pepper
- 1/4 cup instant brown rice

Nutrition Facts Per Serving:
Calories 200, Total Fat 6.8g, Saturated Fat 1.1g, Total Carbs 13.3g, Net Carbs 12.1g, Protein 20.4g, Sugar 4g, Fiber 1.2g, Sodium 1152mg

Instructions:
1. Toss the turkey with the olive oil, balsamic vinegar, basil, and thyme.

2. Season lightly with salt and pepper then cover and chill for 20 minutes.

3. Bring 1/4 cup of water to boil in a small saucepan.

4. Stir in the brown rice then simmer for 5 minutes and remove from heat, covered.

5. Meanwhile, heat a small skillet over medium heat and grease lightly with cooking spray.

6. Add the marinated turkey and sauté for 6 to 8 minutes until cooked through.

7. Spoon the turkey over the brown rice and serve hot.

Chicken Mushroom Stroganoff

Prep Time: 5 minutes
Cook Time: 25 minutes
Servings: 6
Ingredients:

- 1 cup fat-free sour cream
- 2 tablespoons flour
- 1 tablespoon Worcestershire sauce
- 1/2 teaspoon dried thyme
- 1 chicken bouillon cube, crushed
- Salt and pepper
- 1/2 cup water
- 1 medium yellow onion, chopped
- 8 ounces sliced mushrooms
- 1 tablespoon olive oil
- 2 cloves minced garlic
- 12 ounces boneless skinless chicken breast, cooked and shredded
- 6 ounces whole-wheat noodles, cooked

Nutrition Facts Per Serving:
Calories 295, Total Fat 7.8g, Saturated Fat 2g, Total Carbs 29.6g, Net Carbs 26.7g, Protein 24.6g, Sugar 4.7g, Fiber 2.9g, Sodium 225mg

Instructions:

1. Whisk together 2/3 cup of the sour cream with the flour, Worcestershire sauce, thyme, and crushed bouillon in a medium bowl.

2. Season with salt and pepper then slowly stir in the water until well combined.

3. Heat the oil in a large skillet over medium-high heat.

4. Add the onions and mushrooms and sauté for 3 minutes.

5. Stir in the garlic and cook for 2 minutes more then add the chicken.

6. Pour in the sour cream mixture and cook until thick and bubbling.

7. Reduce heat and simmer for 2 minutes.

8. Spoon the chicken and mushroom mixture over the cooked noodles and garnish with the remaining sour cream to serve.

Grilled Tuna Kebabs

Prep Time: 20 minutes
Cook Time: 10 minutes
Servings: 4

Ingredients:
- 2 1/2 tablespoons rice vinegar
- 2 tablespoons fresh grated ginger
- 2 tablespoons sesame oil
- 2 tablespoons soy sauce
- 2 tablespoons fresh chopped cilantro
- 1 tablespoon minced green chile
- 1 1/2 pounds fresh ahi tuna, cut into 1 1/4-inch cubes
- 1 large red pepper, cut into 1-inch pieces
- 1 large red onion, cut into 1-inch pieces

Nutrition Facts Per Serving:
Calories 240, Total Fat 8.2g, Saturated Fat 1g, Total Carbs 8.5g, Net Carbs 6.8g, Protein 31.5g, Sugar 3.4g, Fiber 1.7g, Sodium 503mg

Instructions:

1. Whisk together the rice vinegar, ginger, sesame oil, soy sauce, cilantro, and chili in a medium bowl – add a few drops of liquid stevia extract to sweeten.

2. Toss in the tuna and chill for 20 minutes, covered.

3. Meanwhile, grease a grill pan with cooking spray and soak wooden skewers in water.

4. Slide the tuna cubes onto the skewers with red pepper and onion.

5. Grill for 3 to 4 minutes on each side until done to your liking and serve hot.

Cast-Iron Pork Loin

Prep Time: 10 minutes
Cook Time: 20 minutes
Servings: 6

Ingredients:
- 1 (1 1/2 pounds) boneless pork loin
- Salt and pepper
- 2 tablespoons olive oil
- 2 tablespoons dried herb blend

Nutrition Facts Per Serving:
Calories 205, Total Fat 8.7g, Saturated Fat 2g, Total Carbs 1g, Net Carbs 1g, Protein 29.8g, Sugar 0g, Fiber 0g, Sodium 65mg

Instructions:
1. Heat the oven to 425° F.
2. Trim the excess fat from the pork and season with salt and pepper.
3. Heat the oil in a large cast-iron skillet over medium heat.
4. Add the pork and cook for 2 minutes on each side.
5. Sprinkle the herbs over the pork and transfer to the oven.
6. Roast for 10 to 15 minutes until the internal temperature reaches 145° F.
7. Remove to a cutting board and let rest 5 to 10 minutes before slicing to serve.

Crispy Baked Tofu

Prep Time: 5 minutes
Cook Time: 25 minutes
Servings: 4

Ingredients:
- 1 (14-ounce) block extra-firm tofu
- 1 tablespoon olive oil
- 1 tablespoon cornstarch
- 1/2 teaspoon garlic powder
- Salt and pepper

Nutrition Facts Per Serving:
Calories 140, Total Fat 8.7g, Saturated Fat 1.1g, Total Carbs 2.1g, Net Carbs 2g, Protein 12.7g, Sugar 0.1g, Fiber 0.1g, Sodium 23mg

Instructions:
1. Lay some paper towels out on a flat surface.
2. Cut the tofu into slices up to about 1/2-inch thick and lay them out.
3. Cover the tofu with another paper towel and place a cutting board on top.
4. Let the tofu drain for 10 to 15 minutes.
5. Preheat the oven to 400 °F and line a baking sheet with foil or parchment.
6. Cut the tofu into cubes and place in a large bowl.
7. Toss with the olive oil, cornstarch, garlic powder, salt and pepper until coated.
8. Spread on the baking sheet and bake for 10 minutes.
9. Flip the tofu and bake for another 10 to 15 minutes until crisp. Serve hot.

Tilapia with Coconut Rice

Prep Time: 10 minutes
Cook Time: 15 minutes
Servings: 4

Ingredients:
- 4 (6-ounce) boneless tilapia fillets
- 1 tablespoon ground turmeric
- Salt and pepper
- 1 tablespoon olive oil
- 2 (8.8-ounce) packets precooked whole-grain rice
- 1 cup light coconut milk, shaken
- 1/2 cup fresh chopped cilantro
- 1 1/2 tablespoons fresh lime juice

Nutrition Facts Per Serving:
Calories 460, Total Fat 25.2g, Saturated Fat 15.3g, Total Carbs 27.1g, Net Carbs 23.4g, Protein 34.8g, Sugar 2.4g, Fiber 3.7g, Sodium 145mg

Instructions:
1. Season the fish with turmeric, salt, and pepper.
2. Heat the oil in a large skillet over medium heat and add the fish.
3. Cook for 2 to 3 minutes per side until golden brown.
4. Remove the fish to a plate and cover to keep warm.
5. Reheat the skillet and add the rice, coconut milk, and a pinch of salt.
6. Simmer on high heat until thickened, about 3 to 4 minutes.
7. Stir in the cilantro and lime juice.
8. Spoon the rice onto plates and serve with the cooked fish.

Spicy Turkey Tacos

Prep Time: 5 minutes
Cook Time: 25 minutes
Servings: 8

Ingredients:
- 1 tablespoon olive oil
- 1 medium yellow onion, diced
- 2 cloves minced garlic
- 1 pound 93% lean ground turkey
- 1 cup tomato sauce, no sugar added
- 1 jalapeno, seeded and minced
- 8 low-carb multigrain tortillas

Nutrition Facts Per Serving:
Calories 195, Total Fat 7.8g, Saturated Fat 1.5g, Total Carbs 15.4g, Net Carbs 7.4g, Protein 14.2g, Sugar 1.6g, Fiber 8g, Sodium 380mg

Instructions:
1. Heat the oil in a large skillet over medium heat.

2. Add the onion and sauté for 4 minutes then stir in the garlic and cook 1 minute more.

3. Stir in the ground turkey and cook for 5 minutes until browned, breaking it up with a wooden spoon.

4. Sprinkle on the taco seasoning and cayenne then stir well.

5. Cook for 30 seconds then stir in the tomato sauce and jalapeno.

6. Simmer on low heat for 10 minutes while you warm the tortillas in the microwave.

7. Serve the meat in the tortillas with your favorite taco toppings.

Quick and Easy Shrimp Stir-Fry

Prep Time: 15 minutes
Cook Time: 15 minutes
Servings: 5

Ingredients:

- 1 tablespoon olive oil
- 1 pound uncooked shrimp, peeled and deveined
- Salt and pepper
- 1 tablespoon sesame oil
- 8 ounces snow peas
- 4 ounces broccoli, chopped
- 1 medium red pepper, sliced
- 3 cloves minced garlic
- 1 tablespoon fresh grated ginger
- 1/2 cup soy sauce
- 1 tablespoon cornstarch
- 2 tablespoons fresh lime juice
- 1/4 teaspoon liquid stevia extract

Instructions:

1. Heat the olive oil in a large skillet over medium heat.
2. Add the shrimp and season with salt and pepper then sauté until just pink, about 5 minutes.
3. Remove the shrimp to a bowl and keep warm.
4. Reheat the skillet with the sesame oil and add the veggies.
5. Sauté until the veggies are tender, about 6 to 8 minutes.
6. Stir in the garlic and ginger and cook for 1 minute more.
7. Whisk together the remaining ingredients and pour into the skillet.
8. Toss to coat the veggies then add the shrimp and reheat. Serve hot.

Nutrition Facts Per Serving:

Calories 220, Total Fat 7.4g, Saturated Fat 1.3g, Total Carbs 12.7g, Net Carbs 10.1g, Protein 24.8g, Sugar 3.9g, Fiber 2.6g, Sodium 1670mg

Chicken Burrito Bowl with Quinoa

Prep Time: 15 minutes
Cook Time: 10 minutes
Servings: 6

Ingredients:
- 1 tablespoon chipotle chiles in adobo, chopped
- 1 tablespoon olive oil
- 1/2 teaspoon garlic powder
- 1/2 teaspoon ground cumin
- 1 pound boneless skinless chicken breast
- Salt and pepper
- 2 cups cooked quinoa
- 2 cups shredded romaine lettuce
- 1 cup black beans, rinsed and drained
- 1 cup diced avocado
- 3 tablespoons fat-free sour cream

Nutrition Facts Per Serving:
Calories 410, Total Fat 14.7g, Saturated Fat 3g, Total Carbs 37.4g, Net Carbs 28.9g, Protein 32.4g, Sugar 1.6g, Fiber 8.5g, Sodium 97mg

Instructions:

1. Stir together the chipotle chiles, olive oil, garlic powder, and cumin in a small bowl.

2. Preheat a grill pan to medium-high and grease with cooking spray.

3. Season the chicken with salt and pepper and add to the grill pan.

4. Grill for 5 minutes then flip it and brush with the chipotle glaze.

5. Cook for another 3 to 5 minutes until cooked through.

6. Remove to a cutting board and chop the chicken.

7. Assemble the bowls with 1/6 of the quinoa, chicken, lettuce, beans, and avocado.

8. Top each with a half tablespoon of fat-free sour cream to serve.

Baked Salmon Cakes

Prep Time: 10 minutes
Cook Time: 20 minutes
Servings: 4

Ingredients:
- 15 ounces canned salmon, drained
- 1 large egg, whisked
- 2 teaspoons Dijon mustard
- 1 small yellow onion, minced
- 1 1/2 cups whole-wheat breadcrumbs
- 1/4 cup low-fat mayonnaise
- 1/4 cup nonfat Greek yogurt, plain
- 1 tablespoon fresh chopped parsley
- 1 tablespoon fresh lemon juice
- 2 green onions, sliced thin

Nutrition Facts Per Serving:
Calories 240, Total Fat 12.2g, Saturated Fat 1.4g, Total Carbs 9.3g, Net Carbs 7.8g, Protein 25g, Sugar 1.8g, Fiber 1.5g, Sodium 241mg

Instructions:
1. Preheat the oven to 450°F and line a baking sheet with parchment.
2. Flake the salmon into a medium bowl then stir in the egg and mustard.
3. Mix in the onions and breadcrumbs by hand, blending well, then shape into 8 patties.
4. Grease a large skillet and heat it over medium heat.
5. Add the patties and fry for 2 minutes on each side until browned.
6. Transfer the patties to the baking sheet and bake for 15 minutes or until cooked through.
7. Meanwhile, whisk together the remaining ingredients.
8. Serve the baked salmon cakes with the creamy herb sauce.

Snack & Dessert Recipes

Cinnamon Spiced Popcorn 54
Peanut Butter Banana "Ice Cream" 55
Fruity Coconut Energy Balls 56
Mini Apple Oat Muffins 57
Dark Chocolate Almond Yogurt Cups 58
Chocolate Avocado Mousse 59
Pumpkin Spice Snack Balls 60
Strawberry Lime Pudding Cinnamon 61
Toasted Almonds 62
Grain-Free Berry Cobbler 63
Whole-Wheat Pumpkin Muffins 64

Cinnamon Spiced Popcorn

Prep Time: 10 minutes
Cook Time: 5 minutes
Servings: 4

Ingredients:
- 8 cups air-popped corn
- 2 teaspoons sugar
- 1/2 to 1 teaspoon ground cinnamon
- Butter-flavored cooking spray

Nutrition Facts Per Serving:
Calories 70, Total Fat 0.7g, Saturated Fat 0.1g, Total Carbs 14.7g, Net Carbs 12.2g, Protein 2.1g, Sugar 2.2g, Fiber 2.5g, Sodium 1mg

Instructions:

1. Preheat the oven to 350° F and line a shallow roasting pan with foil.

2. Pop the popcorn using your preferred method.

3. Spread the popcorn in the roasting pan and mix the sugar and cinnamon in a small bowl.

4. Lightly spray the popcorn with cooking spray and toss to coat evenly.

5. Sprinkle with cinnamon and toss again.

6. Bake for 5 minutes until just crisp then serve warm.

Grilled Peaches

Prep Time: 5 minutes
Cook Time: 10 minutes
Servings: 6

Ingredients:
- 6 fresh peaches, ripe
- 1 tablespoon olive oil
- 6 tablespoons fat-free whipped topping

Nutrition Facts Per Serving:
Calories 100, Total Fat 2.7g, Saturated Fat 0.3g, Total Carbs 18g, Net Carbs 15.7g, Protein 1.4g, Sugar 16g, Fiber 2.3g, Sodium 10mg

Instructions:

1. Lightly grease a grill pan and preheat it over medium heat.

2. Cut the peaches in half and remove the pits.

3. Brush the cut sides with olive oil or spritz with cooking spray.

4. Place the peaches cut-side down on the grill for 4 to 5 minutes.

5. Flip the peaches and cook for another 4 to 5 minutes until tender.

6. Spoon the peaches into bowls and serve with fat-free whipped topping.

Peanut Butter Banana "Ice Cream"

Prep Time: 10 minutes
Cook Time: None
Servings: 6

Ingredients:
- 4 medium bananas
- 1/2 cup whipped peanut butter
- 1 teaspoon vanilla extract

Nutrition Facts Per Serving:
Calories 165, Total Fat 8.3g, Saturated Fat 1.8g, Total Carbs 21.4g, Net Carbs 18g, Protein 4.9g, Sugar 11g, Fiber 3.4g, Sodium 74mg

Instructions:
1. Peel the bananas and slice them into coins.
2. Arrange the slices on a plate and freeze until solid.
3. Place the frozen bananas in a food processor.
4. Add the peanut butter and pulse until it is mostly smooth.
5. Scrape down the sides then add the vanilla extract.
6. Pulse until smooth then spoon into bowls to serve.

Fruity Coconut Energy Balls

Prep Time: 15 minutes
Cook Time: None
Servings: 18

Ingredients:
- 1 cup chopped almonds
- 1 cup dried figs
- 1/2 cup dried apricots, chopped
- 1/2 cup dried cranberries, unsweetened
- 1/2 teaspoon vanilla extract
- 1/4 teaspoon ground cinnamon
- 1/2 cup shredded unsweetened coconut

Nutrition Facts Per Serving:
Calories 100, Total Fat 4.9g, Saturated Fat 2.1g, Total Carbs 14.6g, Net Carbs 11.9g, Protein 1.8g, Sugar 10.7g, Fiber 2.7g, Sodium 3mg

Instructions:
1. Place the almonds, figs, apricots, and cranberries in a food processor.
2. Pulse the mixture until finely chopped.
3. Add the vanilla extract and cinnamon then pulse to combine once more.
4. Roll the mixture into 18 small balls by hand.
5. Roll the balls in the shredded coconut and chill until firm.

Mini Apple Oat Muffins

Prep Time: 5minutes
Cook Time: 25 minutes
Servings: 24

Ingredients:
- 1 1/2 cups old-fashioned oats
- 1 teaspoon baking powder
- 1/2 teaspoon ground cinnamon
- 1/4 teaspoon baking soda
- 1/4 teaspoon salt
- 1/2 cup unsweetened applesauce
- 1/4 cup light brown sugar
- 3 tablespoons canola oil
- 3 tablespoons water
- 1 teaspoon vanilla extract
- 1/2 cup slivered almonds

Nutrition Facts Per Serving:
Calories 60, Total Fat 3.1g, Saturated Fat 0.3g, Total Carbs 6.5g, Net Carbs 5.6g, Protein 1.2g, Sugar 2.1g, Fiber 0.9g, Sodium 38mg

Instructions:
1. Preheat the oven to 350 °F and grease a mini muffin pan.
2. Place the oats in a food processor and pulse into a fine flour.
3. Add the baking powder, cinnamon, baking soda, and salt.
4. Pulse until well combined then add the applesauce, brown sugar, canola oil, water, and vanilla then blend smooth.
5. Fold in the almonds and spoon the mixture into the muffin pan.
6. Bake for 22 to 25 minutes until a knife inserted in the center comes out clean.
7. Cool the muffins for 5 minutes then turn out onto a wire rack.

Dark Chocolate Almond Yogurt Cups

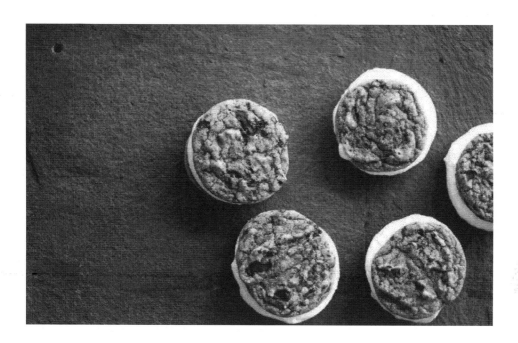

Prep Time: 10 minutes
Cook Time: None
Servings: 6

Ingredients:
- 3 cups plain nonfat Greek yogurt
- 1/2 teaspoon almond extract
- 1/4 teaspoon liquid stevia extract (more to taste)
- 2 ounces 70% dark chocolate, chopped
- 1/2 cup slivered almonds

Nutrition Facts Per Serving:
Calories 170, Total Fat 7.7g, Saturated Fat 2.4g, Total Carbs 11.1g, Net Carbs 8.9g, Protein 14.9g, Sugar 8.1g, Fiber 2.2g, Sodium 41mg

Instructions:
1. Whisk together the yogurt, almond extract, and liquid stevia in a medium bowl.
2. Spoon the yogurt into four dessert cups.
3. Sprinkle with chopped chocolate and slivered almonds.

Chocolate Avocado Mousse

Prep Time: 5 minutes
Cook Time: None
Servings: 3

Ingredients:
- 1 large avocado, pitted and chopped
- 1/4 cup fat-free milk
- 1/4 cup unsweetened cocoa powder (dark)
- 2 teaspoons powdered stevia
- 1 teaspoon vanilla extract
- 2 tablespoons fat-free whipped topping

Nutrition Facts Per Serving:
Calories 180, Total Fat 14.1g, Saturated Fat 3.3g, Total Carbs 13.5g, Net Carbs 6.6g, Protein 3.4g, Sugar 3g, Fiber 6.9g, Sodium 23mg

Instructions:
1. Place the avocado in a food processor and blend smooth.

2. In a small bowl, whisk together the milk and cocoa powder until well combined.

3. Stir in the pureed avocado along with the stevia and vanilla extract.

4. Spoon into bowls and serve with fat-free whipped topping.

Pumpkin Spice Snack Balls

Prep Time: 15 minutes
Cook Time: 10 minutes
Servings: 10

Ingredients:
- 1 1/2 cups old-fashioned oats
- 1/2 cup chopped almonds
- 1/2 cup unsweetened shredded coconut
- 3/4 cup canned pumpkin puree
- 2 tablespoons honey
- 2 teaspoons pumpkin pie spice
- 1/4 teaspoon salt

Nutrition Facts Per Serving:
Calories 170, Total Fat 9.8g, Saturated Fat 6g, Total Carbs 17.8g, Net Carbs 13.7g, Protein 3.8g, Sugar 5.2g, Fiber 4.1g, Sodium 64mg

Instructions:
1. Preheat the oven to 300°F and line a baking sheet with parchment.
2. Combine the oats, almonds, and coconut on the baking sheet.
3. Bake for 8 to 10 minutes until browned, stirring halfway through.
4. Place the pumpkin, honey, pumpkin pie spice, and salt in a medium bowl.
5. Stir in the toasted oat mixture.
6. Shape the mixture into 20 balls by hand and place on a tray.
7. Chill until the balls are firm then serve.

Strawberry Lime Pudding

Prep Time: 15 minutes
Cook Time: 10 minutes
Servings: 4

Ingredients:

- 2 cups plus 2 tablespoons fat-free milk
- 2 teaspoons flavorless gelatin
- 10 large strawberries, sliced
- 1 tablespoon fresh lime zest
- 2 teaspoons vanilla extract
- Liquid stevia extract, to taste

Nutrition Facts Per Serving:

Calories 75, Total Fat 0.4g, Saturated Fat 0.2g, Total Carbs 10.3, Net Carbs 9.2g, Protein 6.3g, Sugar 9.2g, Fiber 1.1g, Sodium 72mg

Instructions:

1. Whisk together 2 tablespoons milk and gelatin in a medium bowl until the gelatin dissolves completely.

2. Place the strawberries in a food processor with the lime juice and vanilla extract.

3. Blend until smooth then pour into a medium bowl.

4. Warm the remaining milk in a small saucepan over medium heat.

5. Stir in the lime zest and heat until steaming (do not boil).

6. Gently whisk the gelatin mixture into the hot milk then stir in the strawberry mixture.

7. Sweeten with liquid stevia to taste and chill until set. Serve cold.

Cinnamon Toasted Almonds

Prep Time: 5 minutes
Cook Time: 25 minutes
Servings: 8

Ingredients:
- 2 cups whole almonds
- 1 tablespoon olive oil
- 1 teaspoon ground cinnamon
- 1/2 teaspoon salt

Nutrition Facts Per Serving:
Calories 150, Total Fat 13.6g, Saturated Fat 1.2g, Total Carbs 5.3g, Net Carbs 2.2g, Protein 5g, Sugar 1g, Fiber 3.1g, Sodium 148mg

Instructions:
1. Preheat the oven to 325°F and line a baking sheet with parchment.
2. Toss together the almonds, olive oil, cinnamon, and salt.
3. Spread the almonds on the baking sheet in a single layer.
4. Bake for 25 minutes, stirring several times, until toasted.

Grain-Free Berry Cobbler

Prep Time: 5 minutes
Cook Time: 25 minutes
Servings: 10

Ingredients:
- 4 cups fresh mixed berries
- 1/2 cup ground flaxseed
- 1/4 cup almond meal
- 1/4 cup unsweetened shredded coconut
- 1/2 tablespoon baking powder
- 1 teaspoon ground cinnamon
- 1/4 teaspoon salt
- Powdered stevia, to taste
- 6 tablespoons coconut oil

Nutrition Facts Per Serving:
Calories 215 Total Fat 16.8g, Saturated Fat 10.4g, Total Carbs 13.1g, Net Carbs 6.7g, Protein 3.7g, Sugar 5.3g, Fiber 6.4g, Sodium 61mg

Instructions:
1. Preheat the oven to 375°F and lightly grease a 10-inch cast-iron skillet.
2. Spread the berries on the bottom of the skillet.
3. Whisk together the dry ingredients in a mixing bowl.
4. Cut in the coconut oil using a fork to create a crumbled mixture.
5. Spread the crumble over the berries and bake for 25 minutes until hot and bubbling.
6. Cool the cobbler for 5 to 10 minutes before serving.

Whole-Wheat Pumpkin Muffins

Prep Time: 15 minutes
Cook Time: 15 minutes
Servings: 36

Ingredients:
- 1 3/4 cup whole-wheat flour
- 1 teaspoon baking powder
- 1 teaspoon baking soda
- 1 teaspoon ground cinnamon
- 1 teaspoon pumpkin pie spice
- 1/2 teaspoon salt
- 2 large eggs
- 1 cup canned pumpkin puree
- 1/3 cup unsweetened applesauce
- 1/4 cup light brown sugar
- 1 teaspoon vanilla extract
- 1/3 cup fat-free milk
- Liquid stevia extract, to taste

Nutrition Facts Per Serving:
Calories 35, Total Fat 0.5g, Saturated Fat 0.1g, Total Carbs 6.4g, Net Carbs 5.7g, Protein 1.3g, Sugar 1.6g, Fiber 0.9g, Sodium 73mg

Instructions:

1. Preheat the oven to 350° F and grease two 24-cup mini muffin pans with cooking spray.

2. Whisk together the flour, baking powder, baking soda, cinnamon, pumpkin pie spice, and salt in a large mixing bowl.

3. In a separate bowl, whisk together the eggs, pumpkin, applesauce, brown sugar, vanilla extract, and milk.

4. Stir the wet ingredients into the dry until well combined.

5. Adjust sweetness to taste with liquid stevia extract, if desired.

6. Spoon the batter into 36 cups and bake for 12 to 15 minutes until cooked through.

Side Dishes

Lemon Garlic Green Beans 67

Rice & Lentil Salad 68

Mashed Butternut Squash 69

Cilantro Lime Quinoa 70
Oven-Roasted Veggies 71

Vegetable Rice Pilaf 72
Curry Roasted Cauliflower
Florets 73
Mushroom Barley Risotto 74

Braised Summer Squash 75

Parsley Tabbouleh 76
Garlic Sautéed Spinach 77

French Lentils

Lemon Garlic Green Beans

Prep Time: 5 minutes
Cook Time: 10 minutes
Servings: 6

Ingredients:
- 1 1/2 pounds green beans, trimmed
- 2 tablespoons olive oil
- 1 tablespoon fresh lemon juice
- 2 cloves minced garlic
- Salt and pepper

Nutrition Facts Per Serving:
Calories 75, Total Fat 4.8g, Saturated Fat 0.7g, Total Carbs 8.5g, Net Carbs 4.6g, Protein 2.1g, Sugar 1.7g, Fiber 3.9g, Sodium 7mg

Instructions:
1. Fill a large bowl with ice water and set aside.
2. Bring a pot of salted water to boil then add the green beans.
3. Cook for 3 minutes then drain and immediately place in the ice water.
4. Cool the beans completely then drain them well.
5. Heat the oil in a large skillet over medium-high heat.
6. Add the green beans, tossing to coat, then add the lemon juice, garlic, salt, and pepper.
7. Sauté for 3 minutes until the beans are tender-crisp then serve hot.

Brown Rice & Lentil Salad

Prep Time: 10 minutes
Cook Time: 10 minutes
Servings: 4

Ingredients:
- 1 cup water
- 1/2 cup instant brown rice
- 2 tablespoons olive oil
- 2 tablespoons red wine vinegar
- 1 tablespoon Dijon mustard
- 1 tablespoon minced onion
- 1/2 teaspoon paprika
- Salt and pepper
- 1 (15-ounce) can brown lentils, rinsed and drained
- 1 medium carrot, shredded
- 2 tablespoons fresh chopped parsley

Nutrition Facts Per Serving:
Calories 145, Total Fat 7.7g, Saturated Fat 1g, Total Carbs 13.1g, Net Carbs 10.9g, Protein 6g, Sugar 1g, Fiber 2.2g, Sodium 57mg

Instructions:
1. Stir together the water and instant brown rice in a medium saucepan.
2. Bring to a boil then simmer for 10 minutes, covered.
3. Remove from heat and set aside while you prepare the salad.
4. Whisk together the olive oil, vinegar, Dijon mustard, onion, paprika, salt, and pepper in a medium bowl.
5. Toss in the cooked rice, lentils, carrots, and parsley.
6. Adjust seasoning to taste then stir well and serve warm.

Mashed Butternut Squash

Prep Time: 5 minutes
Cook Time: 25 minutes
Servings: 6

Ingredients:
- 3 pounds whole butternut squash (about 2 medium)
- 2 tablespoons olive oil
- Salt and pepper

Nutrition Facts Per Serving:
Calories 90, Total Fat 4.8g, Saturated Fat 0.7g, Total Carbs 12.3g, Net Carbs 10.2g, Protein 1.1g, Sugar 2.3g, Fiber 2.1g, Sodium 4mg

Instructions:
1. Preheat the oven to 400°F and line a baking sheet with parchment.
2. Cut the squash in half and remove the seeds.
3. Cut the squash into cubes and toss with oil then spread on the baking sheet.
4. Roast for 25 minutes until tender then place in a food processor.
5. Blend smooth then season with salt and pepper to taste.

Cilantro Lime Quinoa

Prep Time: 5 minutes
Cook Time: 25 minutes
Servings: 6

Ingredients:
- 1 cup uncooked quinoa
- 1 tablespoon olive oil
- 1 medium yellow onion, diced
- 2 cloves minced garlic
- 1 (4-ounce) can diced green chiles, drained
- 1 1/2 cups fat-free chicken broth
- 3/4 cup fresh chopped cilantro
- 1/2 cup sliced green onion
- 2 tablespoons lime juice
- Salt and pepper

Nutrition Facts Per Serving:
Calories 150, Total Fat 4.1g, Saturated Fat 0.5g, Total Carbs 22.5g, Net Carbs 19.8g, Protein 6g, Sugar 1.7g, Fiber 2.7g, Sodium 179mg

Instructions:

1. Rinse the quinoa thoroughly in cool water using a fine mesh sieve.

2. Heat the oil in a large saucepan over medium heat.

3. Add the onion and sauté for 2 minutes then stir in the chile and garlic.

4. Cook for 1 minute then stir in the quinoa and chicken broth.

5. Bring to a boil then reduce heat and simmer, covered, until the quinoa absorbs the liquid – about 20 to 25 minutes.

6. Remove from heat then stir in the cilantro, green onions, and lime juice.

7. Season with salt and pepper to taste and serve hot.

Oven-Roasted Veggies

Prep Time: 5 minutes
Cook Time: 25 minutes
Servings: 6

Ingredients:
- 1 pound cauliflower florets
- 1/2 pound broccoli florets
- 1 large yellow onion, cut into chunks
- 1 large red pepper, cored and chopped
- 2 medium carrots, peeled and sliced
- 2 tablespoons olive oil
- 2 tablespoons apple cider vinegar
- Salt and pepper

Nutrition Facts Per Serving:
Calories 100, Total Fat 5g, Saturated Fat 0.7g, Total Carbs 12.4g, Net Carbs 8.2g, Protein 3.2g, Sugar 5.5g, Fiber 4.2g, Sodium 51mg

Instructions:

1. Preheat the oven to 425° F and line a large rimmed baking sheet with parchment.

2. Spread the veggies on the baking sheet and drizzle with oil and vinegar.

3. Toss well and season with salt and pepper.

4. Spread the veggies in a single layer then roast for 20 to 25 minutes, stirring every 10 minutes, until tender.

5. Adjust seasoning to taste and serve hot.

Vegetable Rice Pilaf

Prep Time: 5 minutes
Cook Time: 25 minutes
Servings: 6

Ingredients:
- 1 tablespoon olive oil
- 1/2 medium yellow onion, diced
- 1 cup uncooked long-grain brown rice
- 2 cloves minced garlic
- 1/2 teaspoon dried basil
- Salt and pepper
- 2 cups fat-free chicken broth
- 1 cup frozen mixed veggies

Nutrition Facts Per Serving:
Calories 90, Total Fat 2.7g, Saturated Fat 0.4g, Total Carbs 12.6g, Net Carbs 10.4g, Protein 3.9g, Sugar 1.5g, Fiber 2.2g, Sodium 143mg

Instructions:

1. Heat the oil in a large skillet over medium heat.

2. Add the onion and sauté for 3 minutes until translucent.

3. Stir in the rice and cook until lightly toasted.

4. Add the garlic, basil, salt, and pepper then stir to combined.

5. Stir in the chicken broth then bring to a boil.

6. Reduce heat and simmer, covered, for 10 minutes.

7. Stir in the frozen veggies then cover and cook for another 10 minutes until heated through. Serve hot.

Curry Roasted Cauliflower Florets

Prep Time: 5 minutes
Cook Time: 25 minutes
Servings: 6

Ingredients:
- 8 cups cauliflower florets
- 2 tablespoons olive oil
- 1 teaspoon curry powder
- 1/2 teaspoon garlic powder
- Salt and pepper

Nutrition Facts Per Serving:
Calories 75, Total Fat 4.9g, Saturated Fat 0.7g, Total Carbs 7.4g, Net Carbs 3.9g, Protein 2.7g, Sugar 3.3g, Fiber 3.5g, Sodium 40mg

Instructions:

1. Preheat the oven to 425 °F and line a baking sheet with foil.

2. Toss the cauliflower with the olive oil and spread on the baking sheet.

3. Sprinkle with curry powder, garlic powder, salt, and pepper.

4. Roast for 25 minutes or until just tender. Serve hot.

Mushroom Barley Risotto

Prep Time: 5 minutes
Cook Time: 25 minutes
Servings: 8

Ingredients:

- 4 cups fat-free beef broth
- 2 tablespoons olive oil
- 1 small onion, diced well
- 2 cloves minced garlic
- 8 ounces thinly sliced mushrooms
- 1/4 tsp dried thyme
- Salt and pepper
- 1 cup pearled barley
- 1/2 cup dry white wine

Nutrition Facts Per Serving:

Calories 155, Total Fat 4.4g, Saturated Fat 0.6g, Total Carbs 21.9g, Net Carbs 17.5g, Protein 5.5g, Sugar 1.2g, Fiber 4.4g, Sodium 455mg

Instructions:

1. Heat the beef broth in a medium saucepan and keep it warm.

2. Heat the oil in a large, deep skillet over medium heat.

3. Add the onions and garlic and sauté for 2 minutes then stir in the mushrooms and thyme.

4. Season with salt and pepper and sauté for 2 minutes more.

5. Add the barley and sauté for 1 minute then pour in the wine.

6. Ladle about 1/2 cup of beef broth into the skillet and stir well to combine.

7. Cook until most of the broth has been absorbed then add another ladle.

8. Repeat until you have used all of the broth and the barley is cooked to al dente.

9. Adjust seasoning to taste with salt and pepper and serve hot.

Braised Summer Squash

Prep Time: 10 minutes
Cook Time: 20 minutes
Servings: 6

Ingredients:
- 3 tablespoons olive oil
- 3 cloves minced garlic
- 1/4 teaspoon crushed red pepper flakes
- 1 pound summer squash, sliced
- 1 pound zucchini, sliced
- 1 teaspoon dried oregano
- Salt and pepper

Nutrition Facts Per Serving:
Calories 90, Total Fat 7.4g, Saturated Fat 1.1g, Total Carbs 6.2g, Net Carbs 4.4g, Protein 1.8g, Sugar 4g, Fiber 1.8g, Sodium 10mg

Instructions:
1. Heat the oil in a large skillet over medium heat.
2. Add the garlic and crushed red pepper and cook for 2 minutes.
3. Add the summer squash and zucchini and cook for 15 minutes, stirring often, until just tender.
4. Stir in the oregano then season with salt and pepper to taste. serve hot.

Parsley Tabbouleh

Prep Time: 5 minutes
Cook Time: 25 minutes
Servings: 6

Ingredients:
- 1 cup water
- 1/2 cup bulgur
- 1/4 cup fresh lemon juice
- 2 tablespoons olive oil
- 2 cloves minced garlic
- Salt and pepper
- 2 cups fresh chopped parsley
- 2 medium tomatoes, died
- 1 small cucumber, diced
- 1/4 cup fresh chopped mint

Nutrition Facts Per Serving:
Calories 110, Total Fat 5.3g, Saturated Fat 0.9g, Total Carbs 14.4g, Net Carbs 10.5g, Protein 3g, Sugar 2.4g, Fiber 3.9g, Sodium 21mg

Instructions:
1. Bring the water and bulgur to a boil in a small saucepan then remove from heat.
2. Cover and let stand until the water is fully absorbed, about 25 minutes.
3. Meanwhile, whisk together the lemon juice, olive oil, garlic, salt, and pepper in a medium bowl.
4. Toss in the cooked bulgur along with the parsley, tomatoes, cucumber, and mint.
5. Season with salt and pepper to taste and serve.

Garlic Sautéed Spinach

Prep Time: 5 minutes
Cook Time: 10 minutes
Servings: 4

Ingredients:
- 1 1/2 tablespoons olive oil
- 4 cloves minced garlic
- 6 cups fresh baby spinach
- Salt and pepper

Nutrition Facts Per Serving:
Calories 60, Total Fat 5.5g, Saturated Fat 0.8g, Total Carbs 2.6g, Net Carbs 1.5g, Protein 1.5g, Sugar 0.2g, Fiber 1.1g, Sodium 36mg

Instructions:

1. Heat the oil in a large skillet over medium-high heat.

2. Add the garlic and cook for 1 minute.

3. Stir in the spinach and season with salt and pepper.

4. Sauté for 1 to 2 minutes until just wilted. Serve hot.

French Lentils

Prep Time: 5 minutes
Cook Time: 25 minutes
Servings: 10

Ingredients:
- 2 tablespoons olive oil
- 1 medium onion, diced
- 1 medium carrot, peeled and diced
- 2 cloves minced garlic
- 1/2 cups water
- 1/4 cups French lentils, rinsed and drained
- 1 teaspoon dried thyme
- 2 small bay leaves
- Salt and pepper

Nutrition Facts Per Serving:
Calories 185, Total Fat 3.3g, Saturated Fat 0.5g, Total Carbs 27.9g, Net Carbs 14.2g, Protein 11.4g, Sugar 1.7g, Fiber 13.7g, Sodium 11mg

Instructions:
1. Heat the oil in a large saucepan over medium heat.
2. Add the onions, carrot, and garlic and sauté for 3 minutes.
3. Stir in the water, lentils, thyme, and bay leaves – season with salt.
4. Bring to a boil then reduce to a simmer and cook until tender, about 20 minutes.
5. Drain any excess water and adjust seasoning to taste. Serve hot.

21 Days Meal Plan

Week 1 Meal Plan (Days 1-7)					
Day	Breakfast	Lunch	Snack or Dessert	Dinner	Calories
1	Herb & Vegetable Egg White Omelet	Chicken Tortilla Soup	Cinnamon Spiced Popcorn	Almond-Crusted Salmon Brown Rice & Lentil Salad	Calories: 1,020 Total Fat: 34.1g Protein: 86.6g Net Carbs: 72.7g
2	Lemon Chia Parfait with Berries	Leftover Chicken Tortilla Soup	Cinnamon Spiced Popcorn	Chicken & Veggie Bowl with Brown Rice	Calories: 1,055 Total Fat: 35g Protein: 84.6g Net Carbs: 81.7g
3	Leftover Lemon Chia Parfait with Berries	Asian Cold Noodle Salad	Grilled Peaches	Leftover Almond-Crusted Salmon Brown Rice & Lentil Salad	Calories: 1,055 Total Fat: 42.5g Protein: 84.2g Net Carbs: 72.4g
4	Whole-Wheat Banana Cinnamon Pancakes	Turkey & Brown Rice Lettuce Cups	Peanut Butter Banana "Ice Cream"	Chicken & Mushroom Stroganoff Lemon Garlic Green Beans	Calories: 1,010 Total Fat: 36.4g Protein: 63.1g Net Carbs: 95.5g
5	Leftover Whole-Wheat Banana Cinnamon Pancakes	Leftover Chicken Tortilla Soup	Grilled Peaches	Leftover Chicken & Veggie Bowl with Brown Rice	Calories: 1,150 Total Fat: 37.6g Protein: 76.3g Net Carbs: 106.9g
6	Denver Omelet Breakfast Salad	Leftover Turkey & Brown Rice Lettuce Cups	Peanut Butter Banana "Ice Cream"	Leftover Chicken & Mushroom Stroganoff Lemon Garlic Green Beans	Calories: 1,125 Total Fat: 51.9g Protein: 85.4g Net Carbs: 67.7g
7	Leftover Whole-Wheat Banana Cinnamon Pancakes	Asian Cold Noodle Salad	Cinnamon Spiced Popcorn	Leftover Chicken & Mushroom Stroganoff Lemon Garlic Green Beans	Calories: 1,020 Total Fat: 31.7g Protein: 62.5g Net Carb: 105.6g

Week 2 Meal Plan (Days 8 - 14)					
Day	Breakfast	Lunch	Snack or Dessert	Dinner	Calories
8	Fruit and Nut Granola	Chicken, Spinach, and Pesto Soup	Fruity Coconut Energy Balls (2)	Beef Fajitas	Calories: 1,005 Total Fat: 47.6g Protein: 69.3g Net Carbs: 60.5g
9	Easy Egg Scramble	Shrimp & Black Bean Salad	Dark Chocolate Almond Yogurt Cups	Sautéed Turkey Bowl Mashed Butternut Squash	Calories: 1,035 Total Fat: 38.9g Protein: 83.4g Net Carbs: 72.3g
10	Leftover Fruit and Nut Granola	Leftover Chicken, Spinach, and Pesto Soup	Fruity Coconut Energy Balls (2)	Leftover Beef Fajitas	Calories: 1,005 Total Fat: 47.6g Protein: 69.3g Net Carbs: 60.5g
11	Eggs Baked in Peppers	Creamy Broccoli Chicken Salad	Grain-Free Berry Cobbler	Grilled Tuna Kebabs Vegetable Rice Pilaf	Calories: 1,045 Total Fat: 49.3g Protein: 74.1g Net Carbs: 59.5g
12	Leftover Eggs Baked in Peppers	Leftover Shrimp & Black Bean Salad	Dark Chocolate Almond Yogurt Cups	Leftover Grilled Tuna Kebabs Vegetable Rice Pilaf	Calories: 1,165 Total Fat: 44.4g Protein: 104.2g Net Carbs: 71.6g
13	Leftover Eggs Baked in Peppers	Leftover Chicken, Spinach, and Pesto Soup	Fruity Coconut Energy Balls (3)	Crispy Baked Tofu French Lentils	Calories: 1,075 Total Fat: 56g Protein: 70g Net Carbs: 67.3g
14	Banana Matcha Breakfast Smoothie	Leftover Creamy Broccoli Chicken Salad	Grain-Free Berry Cobbler	Leftover Crispy Baked Tofu French Lentils	Calories: 1,010 Total Fat: 34.5g Protein: 54.6g Net Carbs: 87.2g

Day	Breakfast	Lunch	Snack or Dessert	Dinner	Calories
15	Easy Vegetable Frittata	Carrot Ginger Soup	Mini Apple Oat Muffins (3)	Cast-Iron Pork Loin Oven-Roasted Veggies French Lentils	Calories: 1,100 Total Fat: 53g Protein: 72.6g Net Carbs: 59.8g
16	Leftover Easy Vegetable Frittata	Chickpea, Tuna, and Kale Salad	Chocolate Avocado Mousse	Leftover Cast-Iron Pork Loin Oven-Roasted Veggies French Lentils	Calories: 1,190 Total Fat: 54.8g Protein: 88.5g Net Carbs: 59.6g
17	Spiced Overnight Oats	Leftover Carrot Ginger Soup	Mini Apple Oat Muffins (3)	Tilapia with Coconut Rice Oven-Roasted Veggies	Calories: 1,005 Total Fat: 50.2g Protein: 53.6g Net Carbs: 72.4
18	Herb & Vegetable Egg White Omelet	Grilled Avocado Hummus Paninis	Mini Apple Oat Muffins (4)	Spicy Turkey Tacos Cilantro Lime Quinoa Oven-Roasted Veggies	Calories: 1,015 Total Fat: 40.9g Protein: 52.2g Net Carbs: 83.2g
19	Leftover Spiced Overnight Oats	Leftover Grilled Avocado Hummus Paninis	Cinnamon Toasted Almonds	Leftover Tilapia with Coconut Rice Oven-Roasted Veggies	Calories: 1,080 Total Fat: 62.1g Protein: 57.1g Net Carbs: 63.4g
20	Leftover Easy Vegetable Frittata	Leftover Carrot Ginger Soup	Mini Apple Oat Muffins (4)	Leftover Spicy Turkey Tacos Cilantro Lime Quinoa	Calories: 1,015 Total Fat: 51g Protein: 49.6g Net Carbs: 69.2g
21	Leftover Spiced Overnight Oats	Chickpea, Tuna, and Kale Salad	Cinnamon Toasted Almonds and Chocolate Avocado Mousse	Leftover Spicy Turkey Tacos Cilantro Lime Quinoa	Calories: 1,030 Total Fat: 47.3 Protein: 56.7g Net Carbs: 70g

Made in the USA
San Bernardino, CA
21 February 2020